Married for Five Minutes

Hope for Living Inside Real-Life Marriages

Shundria Riddick, M.A., LPC
and Michelle Stimpson

Sis. Lois,

Marriage Works!

Shundria

ISBN 1-943563-05-5
Library of Congress Control Number: 2016906301

Published by MLStimpson Enterprises
P.O. Box 1592
Cedar Hill, TX 75104

The stories included in this book are works of fiction. The commentary is not intended to be diagnostic for the reader or replace therapy.

Printed in the United States of America
Cover Design by Michelle Stimpson
Edited by Paulette Nunlee, FiveStarProofing

Kudos for Married for Five Minutes

Forget about buying another casserole dish from the registry. My soon-to-be-married friends will be getting beautifully wrapped copies of this book! I so could have benefited from this book when I married five years ago.

NiaShanta Ross - Author of *Worth the Wait*

I smiled as I read because it brought to mind couples I have coached through some of these experiences. With biblical marriage still under attack, this book will bring much needed hope and encouragement to couples.

Dena Crecy – Life Purpose Coach;
Relationships God-Style www.RGSCoachingCenter.org

This book will become the seed planted within marriages that will be watered with prayer that will make way for the increase God intended for husbands and wives.

Dr. Linda F. Beed - Author, Speaker; www.LindaBeed.com

Many of the books I've read I've skimmed through and rushed to the end. This book kept me engaged and anticipating the resolutions from the counseling comments. The reading was fluid and pragmatic. The counselor's comments are beneficial to readers regardless of their relationship status.

Desrie Perry McCoy - Reviewer

Dedication

For couples facing tough seasons—
Hold on to His promises alone.
They never fail.

Acknowledgments

Shundria:

With mounds of awe and gratefulness, I thank Jesus Christ for standing on the water and telling me to jump out of the boat. Lord, your loving kindness is better than life. You were right. I didn't drown!

Chris, my wonderful husband, I would have never gotten this far without your words of encouragement. Thank you for the honest critiques and loving me to my best. I love this life with you—Proverbs 17:17. To my son Joshua, thank you for making my heart smile when you called me cool for writing a book. Elyana, my sweet girl, thank you for screaming and jumping for joy with me when we said it was finished. My baby boy Noah, thank you for your sweet hugs and kisses as you passed by while I sat at my computer. You guys will always be my babies.

Thanks to my sister Desrie and my parents, Lois and Roy, for believing in me. To my Tribe, thank you for cheering for me. A special thank you to Chrystal Hurst for late night writing, and coffee and pancakes at 2:00 a.m. You loved on me and I am grateful. Your love for books and gab makes my inner nerd happy.

Finally, Michelle, thank you for believing in me. Your grace, love, generosity, and support are overwhelming. I am forever changed and much obliged.

Michelle:

Thank You, Lord, for answering the prayers about my marriage with responses that glorify You rather than simply make my life more convenient and self-serving. You always know what is best.

Thanks to my husband Stevie for being exactly who he is. I love you, Babe. I appreciate you more and more each day.

Thank you to Karen Bradford (also a part of the launch team), whose timely, God-inspired, Titus 2 intervention saved my marriage. *For real* for real. Had you not grabbed me by my shoulders, looked into my eyes, and told me some stuff about what God wanted to do in my marriage if I opened myself to Him, this book wouldn't exist. I'm forever grateful. And I'm honored to do the same for others.

Thank you to my readers, my Facebook family, bloggers, and all those who continue to spread the word about the works the Lord gives me. I'm honored to know you all.

Shundria and Michelle:

Thank you Paulette Nunlee for lending your editing expertise. Miriam Glover, thanks for the press release! We appreciate you ladies!

Special thanks from both of us to our online launch team: April Dishon Barker, Dr. Linda F. Beed, Jeanetta Britt, Tonie Butler, Alicia Castile, Tamara Davis, Shileen Esguerra, Shannon Green, Kendra Norman Holmes, Gwen Hughes, Norma Jarrett, Stephanie Johnson,Tiffany Johnson, Eugenea King, Crystal Levingston, Michelle

Lindo-Rice, Lynelle Logan, CaSandra Marshall-McLaughlin, Alice Mayfield, Tia Webster McCollors, Desrie McCoy, Tiara Byrd Moore, Danielle Nicole Moss, Chinedu Okafor, Shironaka Reese, Re Richardson, Mira Rollins, NiaShanta Ross, Chandra Shaw, Holly Spivey, Adrian Williams, and Sherry Williams. Just knowing we had 30+ people willing to dedicate their time to helping us get started was amazingly encouraging. God bless!

Foreword by Chrystal Evans Hurst
Bestselling Author of *Kingdom Woman*

What do you get when you put a seasoned writer with a gift for drawing readers into an engaging story with an esteemed counselor and therapist with a gift for helping the reader gain perspective, believe for the best, and experience rising hope?

You get one great book.

Both Michelle Stimpson and Shundria Riddick know how to dive deep and get to the heart of the matter when they write, when they speak, and when they engage with others one-on-one.

Especially when it comes to marriage.

Having known these ladies personally for many years, I'm excited to see them put their experiences, knowledge, and heart into written form so that others can know that they are not alone, that someone understands, and that there are practical solutions for being married and *thriving* in marriage.

The stories here will engage you. The practically tangible and palpable illustrations will connect with you on a deep level as Michelle and Shundria talk about scenarios many of us have experienced first hand. But you will also receive tools to handle situations in your own marriage with authority, strength, grace, and understanding from women who get where you are coming from.

While the narratives in this book acknowledge the

reality of what we married women have in common or what marital pangs or disappointments we may share, Michelle and Shundria offer guidance within these pages so that you can transcend your current frustrations and move towards clarity and commitment for what you can do to encourage yourself and encourage your man.

How do I know that this is true?

I've had both of these women encourage me in my own marriage. They have helped me look at the relationship I have with my husband and gain a new perspective. I have learned how to examine the difficult conditions from more than just my own viewpoint. I have learned to see my own selfishness but also to recognize the responsibility that I have to care for my own soul. Most of all, I have realized—time and time again—that I'm not alone and there are many women who have faced what I've faced and handled it well.

So much of the writing process is figuring out what to say, but these two have a wealth of information about life and love with which to encourage, teach, and sustain you because they've been sharing with women on the subject of marriage for a long time. The "what" along with the needed "whys" and "hows" have now made their way onto pages that you and I can glean from—over and over again.

Both Michelle and Shundria use the principles they share in this book in their own marriages. They know what works. It's a blessing to see them share their wisdom with this labor of love as an overflow of the blessing that they have already been to so many women that have crossed their paths...

Starting with me.

Contents

Part 3: Expectations

Part 4: Family Dynamics

Introduction

Recently I (Michelle) had lunch with a newlywed friend of mine. She and I have known each other about six years—four years before she married, two after. This was one of our "Girl, I need help" conversations, which have become more frequent since she has taken on the roles of wife, stepmother to a preteen daughter, and caregiver for her own mom.

Since we'd had our fair share of let-it-all-out sessions, I had to stop her in the middle of her vent to ask, "But wait! Didn't I tell you marriage was hard before you got married?"

She sighed. "Yes. Everybody said that, but then they'd talk about stuff like leaving the toilet seat up, which isn't a big deal. Plus, I guess I thought if I picked the right person, *my* marriage wouldn't be *that* hard."

I submitted to her (and you, reader) that any time two imperfect people enter into an agreement to imitate Christ's perfect love for us, there will be...shall we say...shortcomings. Small shortcomings. Epic shortcomings. But definitely, shortcomings. Daily.

And while this "gap" between the ideal and reality is often painfully discouraging, we are never more like Him than when we choose to love an imperfect person despite the fact that they may be acting unlovable at the moment. This is the love God has for us through Christ, the perfect illustration of His grace toward us, which is new every morning.

Shundria and I decided there are already plenty of books addressing issues placing a marriage in immediate crisis, namely addiction, adultery, and physical abuse. We wanted to focus on the issues that aren't necessarily blatant deal-breakers but that, over time, subtly cause wear-and-tear on a marriage—the kinds of things when left unchecked, turn into deep-seated resentment and make a person feel like getting married was their worst mistake.

We know this feeling. We've been there. We've done that. In fact, despite our forty plus combined years of matrimony, both of us experienced this feeling multiplied by 100 as we were writing this manuscript. Through our transparent discussions and note comparisons, we began to recognize the patterns of attack, offer encouragement and prayer, and edify one another in Christ. Thank God we had each other to share our frustrations and receive encouragement from one another.

Unfortunately, many of us are afraid or unable to connect with people at a level deep enough to feel comfortable exposing ourselves. Or we may be reluctant to share our spouse's frailties, because we truly don't want to throw them under the bus. Even if we did open up, how could we know that the other person is being honest, too, since we can't be a fly on the wall at their home?

A word to our unmarried sisters—we don't want to scare you away from walking down the aisle! We do actually like being married and would do it all over again if given the choice. Please don't be intimidated by these scenarios. Marriage is good. We just want you to know that there's more to marital conflict than someone squeezing the toothpaste in the middle or sleeping with the television on. Vowing to love someone without knowing exactly what that might look like in the future takes a great deal of faith, no matter how much two people love each other as they walk down the aisle. Trust in God. He is faithful. Do things His way and He will be glorified.

We pray that as each reader spends five minutes inside other couple's issues, they will be able to rest assured the bumps and bruises encountered in their own relationship might be more common to *all* marriages than they thought.

We pray that the "Counselor's Commentary" following each vignette will enable you to view the issues from a different perspective. Even if your perspective doesn't change, we hope that you will at least take comfort in the fact you are not the first person to deal with deep challenges in a marriage. Nor will you be the last. Conflict is a part of every deep human relationship, and marriage is not an all-or-nothing deal. At some point, every married believer comes to the conclusion that their union won't ever be perfect—but it *can* get better as they walk selflessly and grow in the knowledge of God.

I (Shundria) believe that most of the couples in these scenarios would benefit from Christian counseling. I hope that my responses to their dilemmas will shed enough light to point you in the right direction if you're facing a similar situation. For continued support, seek the Lord and ask Him to pair you and your spouse with someone who might help you learn how to improve your marriage.

Above all, we pray that Christ be glorified as we look to Him, our ultimate Groom, Who has committed Himself to loving us no matter what.

In His Love,

Shundria Riddick

Michelle Stimpson

Part 1

I Married a Human Being

1 - Angry Spouse

Couple: Alyssa and Brian Kimbrough
Married: 14 years
Children: McKayla – age 14
Other: Two dogs

"Bye, Alyssa. Have a great weekend!" Jamie, her co-worker, sang as she headed past Alyssa's bright, spacious corner office.

"You, too." Alyssa waved at Jamie's back, imagining what a 'great weekend' must be in Jamie's world. Maybe a picnic at the park or a fun night at the movies with friends or her boyfriend.

Unlike Jamie's probably spectacular weekend, Friday through Sunday at the Kimbrough household consisted mainly of Alyssa going to McKayla's dance competitions and practices. Alyssa was dedicated to McKayla's dance career, which they hoped would lead to college scholarships and maybe even a glamorous career as a professional performing artist. Sports teams, Vegas, Broadway—all viable options for a young lady as talented as McKayla.

Alyssa packed her attaché with a few client files and headed home to make dinner before McKayla and Brian arrived, and before she and her daughter had to attend the evening's practices. The dance troupe usually rehearsed longer on Friday nights.

An hour later, Alyssa finished the spaghetti and took the bread from the oven. The mouthwatering aroma of garlic and butter filled her nostrils. Her mom used to cook like this seven days a week...before she was killed by a drunk driver when Alyssa was a senior in college.

Her mom, stolen from her. Just like that.

Alyssa heard the door swing open and waited to determine who was entering. A few seconds later, Alyssa was certain it was Brian because she'd heard the car keys slam on the coffee table. She heard the grunting as he took off his work boots. And not a word had been spoken to her.

If he doesn't want to talk to me, I don't want to talk to him, either.

Alyssa made herself a plate and sat at the kitchen table. She blessed her food, then began enjoying the scrumptious meal all by herself. Today was just like any other day in their household.

Brian showered and then came back to the living room. Alyssa could see his feet elevated in his favorite lounge chair.

After finishing her meal, she rinsed her plate, fork, and glass at the sink.

Brian entered the kitchen. "Spaghetti again?" He opened the refrigerator. "What else is there to eat?"

Alyssa refused to answer. *Jerk.* She loaded her dishes into the sink.

"You deaf?"

If only I were so lucky. "You don't have to eat the spaghetti if you don't want to."

"You wouldn't have to cook only spaghetti if you'd take a class and learn how to cook something else. My mom cooked a ton of different things. Steak, chicken, veal. Not just *spaghetti.*"

"My mom cooked a lot of things, too, before she died," Alyssa cut him off.

Brian closed the refrigerator door. He rolled his eyes as he made his way toward the pot of spaghetti, plate in hand. "Are you going to use that excuse forever?"

"It's not an excuse!"

"It *is* when the incident happened more than fifteen years ago. You're a big girl now. And I do mean *big* girl." He chuckled slightly. "I don't know how you keep gaining weight when all you cook is stuff from the kids' menu at restaurants." He piled his plate with spaghetti and took a forkful into his mouth. "Needs more salt."

Brian grabbed the salt from the pantry and shook seasoning onto his plate. "If you're going to make one dish over and over again, at least get it right."

I can't stand you. I wish I'd never met you. The words were right on the tip of her tongue, but she couldn't bring herself to speak them. She'd seen Brian angry before. Really angry. And it wasn't pretty. He hadn't hit her, but he'd gotten all up in her face, yelling and screaming that no woman was going to disrespect him in his own home.

Instead, Alyssa left the kitchen. She went to her bedroom, and waited for McKayla to come home so she could escape the negative, hateful words of the man who'd promised before God and witnesses to "cherish" her.

What a joke.

Angry Spouses
Counselor's Commentary

When we enter marriage, our hearts are full of expectations. Although we might have participated in premarital counseling, read books, attended many conferences, and been told about the issues in marriages, we still created lofty expectations and required our spouses to fulfill those dreams. Sure you mention what you want in marriage. But the magnitude of the expectations is far greater than you yourself can even express. Unbeknownst to your spouse, they are being held responsible for responses or behaviors they are unaware of. Truth be told: Many of us aren't even aware of the depth of expectation until we enter the marriage and become disappointed in our spouses when we feel that our needs aren't met. Rarely do we search within ourselves to identify the root of our expectations. If we did, we would realize that many of them began before we'd met the *one* we have vowed to love until death do us part.

Some expectations entering marriage are due to falling in love with the potential of our mates. We see some sign of them having the ability to be responsible, nurturing, honor commitment, and pursue productivity without actually witnessing the evidence. Some of us may even think we can love this potential into materialization. If they never meet this potential or indicate an unwillingness to work toward fulfillment, frustration sets in and feeds anger until it grows into resentment. It is unreasonable to expect love to change an individual when they are not motivated to make the choices for themselves.

How we are parented, our childhood experiences, adulthood experiences, dating, biblical knowledge, etc., have all formed our expectations of the marital relationship and our spouses. Deciding if they are appropriate does not become part of our thought processes until they are not met, questioned or challenged. We rarely run them through prayer to examine whether they are appropriate or selfish in nature.

In Alyssa and Brian's situation, it appears there are feelings of disappointment that have led to anger and a need to retaliate towards each other. Alyssa may have needs associated with Brian's lack of compassion regarding her losing her mother. Brian may have needs associated with feeling like he does not get enough attention from Alyssa since she has all but devoted her life to McKayla's potential dance career. He may also feel disrespected and unneeded in his own household. As a result of both spouses' unmet needs, the evidence of this disappointment can be heard in their sarcasm and seemingly constant need to insult each other. Unknowingly they are communicating to their daughter this disappointment which negatively impacts her relationship with them both. McKayla will likely develop a propensity towards anger and poor expectations in her relationships with men.

The thing about anger is that it's never what it appears to be. Anger is actually a secondary emotion. Something happened that triggered a feeling. The feeling was then followed by anger. Anger can be expressed as depression, retaliation, sarcasm, bitterness, etc. We must examine what initiated the feeling in order to address the root issue.

Alyssa and Brian have rehearsed their disappointment of the other so often in their thoughts, they've justified the mistreatment of each other. Each has failed to realize that in hurting the other, they are damaging the relationship both are responsible for nurturing.

Communicating the feelings of hurt and disappointment is vital to establishing a healthier relationship. Although it is important to express these expectations, it is also important to examine them. *Is what I'm asking of my spouse appropriate? Is it selfish? Am I expecting behavior that we've never demonstrated? Am I expecting my spouse to heal a hurt that only God can heal? Am I placing the responsibility for my happiness solely on my spouse? Am I willing to give to my spouse what I am expecting from him?*

It is essential that both Brian and Alyssa cease from feeding their anger with thoughts of disappointment and frustration. This can be addressed through routine self-exploration. Continuing to validate their enmity only clouds their eagerness to meet each other's needs—an eagerness that could provide healing and restoration. If their attempts of self-exploration prove difficult and ineffective, it is important that they seek the assistance of a counselor. Through professional guidance, both can address inappropriate expectations and negative thinking that have infiltrated their relationship.

2 - Possibly Addicted Spouse

Couple: Joel and Monica McKinney
Married: 8 years

After a long but informative morning meeting about employee benefits, Joel checked the email messages on his phone.

Alert from Chase: Your Account Ending in x2887 is Overdrawn.

Quickly, he opened the message and read that the checking account he shared with his wife, Monica, was sitting at -$82.33 thanks to a bounced check and an Insufficient Funds fee.

How can this be?

He clicked to read a detailed transaction report.

"Joel, aren't you going to lunch with us?" Janet, his supervisor, asked.

In light of what he'd just seen on the screen, he had to decline by shaking his head.

Nathan, the newest member of their IT team prodded, "Oh, come on! We're going to that new Mexican restaurant on Main."

How could Joel tell his boss and co-workers he was too broke to go out for a simple lunch? "No, thanks. I think...my stomach didn't agree with my breakfast," he lied. He rubbed his midsection for effect.

"Okay. Next time?"

"Yeah. You guys go ahead. I'll see you after lunch."

With his co-workers out of the room and the presenter packing up her materials, Joel was free to review the latest transactions and figure out what had caused their account to go into the red.

It didn't take long to find the culprit. Just below the deduction for the church tithe was a purchase from *Big Daddy's Liquor. $32.87.*

His insides boiled with anger even as he dialed Monica's work number.

"It's a great day at Smith Middle School. This is Mrs. Ringhowser. How may I help you?"

Joel feigned a pleasant voice. "Hello, Mrs. Ringhowser, this is Mr. McKinney. I'm trying to reach Monica."

"Well, she's on lunch duty right now. Central Office has asked all the principals to keep a watch on the cafeterias the week before spring break. Kids get rowdy and all, you know?" The woman laughed jovially.

TMI. "I understand, but I really need to speak to her," Joel insisted.

"I suppose I could call her on the walkie-talkie if you'd like."

"Yes, thank you. I would appreciate that very much."

Through his peripheral vision, Joel could see the presenter wave good-bye. Again, he faked a bright smile. "Thanks for everything."

Several minutes later, his wife's voice came through the phone. "This is Mrs. McKinney, how can I help you?"

"It's me."

"Oh. Kathy didn't say it was—"

"Good thing she *didn't* say it was me because you probably wouldn't have picked up the phone. What in the world is going on with you? You spent another thirty-something dollars at Big Daddy's yesterday. A Wednesday, Monica. It's the middle of the work-week, for crying out loud. Why on earth would you need to spend thirty-two dollars on liquor? And now we're in the negative because we had a fee. Who writes a check for liquor anyway? Who does that? Answer me!"

He heard his wife sigh. "Just move money from the savings account. It's no big deal. If you'd make the savings the back-up like I told you to, we wouldn't have this problem."

"We wouldn't have this problem if you had control over your drinking."

"I'm gonna hang up the phone now."

"Monica, don't you—"

It was too late already. Thanks to an old-fashioned landline at the campus, Joel had literally heard her hang up the phone.

He stared at the mobile phone in his hand. Bewildered. Wondering what on earth had transpired. If Monica

31

thought the answer to the problem was simply to move money around, she was crazy.

And if she thought he was going to sit by and let her ruin his life the way his own mother had destroyed his father through alcoholism, Monica was sadly mistaken. He'd leave her long before he'd travel down that destructive road with her.

Possibly Addicted Spouse
Counselor's Commentary

When we get married we all understand that we will deal with difficult situations. We're told in premarital counseling, and by family and friends that hard times happen. We expect them. And we chose the one we married to share these hard times with. Some of us have been through hard times with our mates, overcome the difficulties, and established a deeper connection with them as a result.

But sometimes, it doesn't happen that way.

Unfortunately in this situation, Joel is now faced with a problem his wife doesn't think is an issue. What should he do? Should he accuse her of addiction? Should he open a new bank account and start to remove himself slowly from their marriage?

Joel noted that he would not allow his wife to ruin his life like his mother ruined his father's. Should he call for her family to have an intervention? After all, she is buying alcohol on a Wednesday and overdrawing the account.

At this point, Joel should take a deep breath and not jump to any conclusions. He has quickly given his wife a diagnosis of alcoholism, accused her of ruining his life, and considered leaving her over a check to Big Daddy's and an overdrawn bank account.

Let's back up and deal with Joel's baggage first. Many of us have had experiences in our childhood we have vowed to never allow to enter our adult lives and especially not in our marriages. We are determined not to be our mothers, aunts or grandmothers. Nonetheless, many of us are not very successful fulfilling these promises to ourselves. We run so hard and fast to be different but find ourselves with the exact same problems. Why? We underestimate the power of our childhood environment and learned behavior. We spend our formative years learning to relate and communicate in our family structures.

We usually identify in early adulthood that we need to change, but we often don't know how. So we usually run towards the familiar. If we have an alcoholic father, we have learned how to love an alcoholic or someone who has the propensity to become an addict. We have been thoroughly trained to love, support, and excuse disturbing behaviors and red flags, because usually these things are seen as normal.

Strangely, it is a place of familiarity and comfort. In some instances we identify these red flags, but we tend to convince ourselves that we can handle it. We can fix it by loving them through it. We can teach them to be different. We think that once they see how much they are damaging the relationship, they will stop. They will choose us and not their addiction. They love us, don't they?

It's the great expectation of marriage that both will choose love for the other to overcome anything. Unfortunately, the divorce rate suggests that too often we make the wrong choice.

In this particular situation, it will be beneficial to Joel to find clarity and perspective because of his history. His fearful concern about the possible direction the marriage is heading is usually verbalized and presented as anger and accusation. He needs to open the lines of communication with Monica from the standpoint of trying to gain insight regarding her behaviors.

This is not to say he should ignore his concerns and only focus on her possibly having a problem. It's also not a reason to address her as a victim that he must rescue. Instead, he must obtain an explanation from his wife with the intention of getting an understanding and not gathering information to support his own prescribed diagnosis. Accusing and diagnosing Monica at this point of anything other than being financially irresponsible is premature and hurtful to both of them.

Speaking his truth to his wife is uncomfortable and scary. Joel shouldn't avoid these feelings but realize they come with talking to Monica about her behavior. It is important that he does not flood her with his emotions and accusations. He should keep his conversation simple and truthful. He might simply state, "I have noticed increased spending on alcohol that has affected our account. It really upsets me when I find out that you have not been honest about your drinking."

He must avoid adding any more feelings or bombarding her with lists of events, hurts, and fears. This will often increase defensiveness and result in intense arguments that will eventually dismantle any efforts toward addressing a possible addiction or irresponsible spending, leaving both with feelings of frustration, loneliness, and being unsupported.

He should allow room for his wife to address his concerns. Any expectation of immediate acceptance of responsibility or swift change is irrational and will result in disappointment. It is necessary that Joel's goal in the conversation mainly be to voice his concern of how her behavior is affecting him and their marriage. It is not for him to accuse, diagnose, or get a confession.

Simple and honest communication from Joel regarding his experience may be met with defensiveness, but initially he is only voicing his current experience and how it is affecting him. There is no need to retaliate. Alcoholism breeds on conflict, arguments, chaos, and dishonesty. It is rendered lifeless in peace and truth.

Let's be honest, if all difficult conversations were easy and ended in compliance we would not have so many ongoing issues. If Joel's fear of alcoholism is realized, it is important that he reaches out to a professional who can guide him in his attempts to address it. He is ill-equipped to solve it alone and will have a tendency to infuse his own childhood experiences and attempt to solve them through his genuine support of his wife. He needs the support of those who are knowledgeable, empathic, and skilled in this area. Above all, Joel must remember that he is fighting the enemy of addiction, not his wife.

3 – Snoring

(An Excerpt from *Did I Marry the Wrong Guy?* By Michelle Stimpson)

Couple: Stevie and Michelle Stimpson
Married: 17 years at the time
Children: Steven – age 17, daughter Kalen – age 12

Michelle: It is with a somber face and complete sincerity that I dedicate an entire chapter of this book to the problem of snoring. Yes, I know there are dozens of things a person can do to irritate one's spouse. But snoring absolutely takes the cake for me—or at least it used to.

Once, when Stevie and I were dating, we were at his parents' house watching television in the living room, about 35 feet away from the hallway leading to the bedrooms. As we watched television, I heard this loud, grating sound emanating from one of the rooms. And yet, my then-boyfriend kept watching television as though he didn't hear this noise.

Well, I didn't want to be rude, but this mysterious racket was getting so loud, I almost couldn't hear the TV. So, I asked, "Why is your brother in his room roaring?" I honestly thought maybe his brother was in there practicing for a role in *The Lion King*.

Stevie replied, "That's not my brother. That's my dad. Snoring."

I had never heard anyone snore like that in my life! I didn't even know it was possible to snore so loudly that other people in other rooms of a house could *feel* it.

Annoyed, I asked Stevie if we could leave. Little did I know, months later I'd find out that the snoring apple doesn't fall far from the tree.

This is hard to even write, but I'll admit: for the first eight years of our marriage, Stevie and I rarely slept in the same bed at night. We might have started off in the same bed, but at some point during the night, one of us would have to leave. We had two small kids and I was teaching middle and high school full time; there was no way on earth I could function without sleep.

I resented Stevie for snoring. He resented me waking him up in the middle of the night. He accused me of waking him up for no reason; I accused him of being an exceptionally obnoxious snorer. I even recorded him snoring once so he could hear how loud he was. He said I probably had the volume up too high, plus it wasn't his fault I was a light sleeper.

Stevie tried nose strips, but they wouldn't stick because his nose sweats at night. He also tried some contraption that set his jaw differently, but he said it was uncomfortable. I tried earplugs, but they didn't stop the bonus snoring vibration effect. Sometimes, I took NyQuil to knock myself out. The NyQuil did work, but then there's the whole drugging-myself thing, which I figured probably wasn't a good long-term plan.

After nearly a decade of this midnight bed-shuffle, I was talking to a newlywed girlfriend of mine and confessed our weird sleeping arrangements. She said, "Y'all gotta do something, girl. That's not normal. It's got to be affecting your marriage."

Light bulb moment. I had never considered the fact that arguing in the middle of the night followed by sleeping in separate beds might be impacting our marriage. *Duh!* Still, I didn't know what to do about it.

Somehow, some way, it occurred to me to pray about the situation. But what was I supposed to pray? *God help my husband stop snoring? God make me sleep like a drunk person?* Was this whole thing somebody's fault? Was there a scripture on snoring?

Though I was unclear of what to pray, I took the matter before God in a jumble of confused words. Thank God He knows how to make sense of our mess.

I can't tell you exactly when God changed the situation, but He did. One morning, I woke up in my bed next to my husband and thought, *That's weird. We slept in the same bed together all night, and I didn't even have to tell him to turn over.* And then it happened again the next morning. The next night, one of us left the bedroom because of snoring. But then on morning four, I was still in my bed next to Stevie. Before I knew it, God had changed the situation. I'm not sure whether He lowered the volume on Stevie's snoring or if He made my ears less sensitive to it. I wish I could explain what happened—especially since this is an informational book and all—but I can't. I just know He did *something* to fix the situation.

Years later, we faced another uprisal of the snoring. My husband went to see a doctor and learned he had sleep apnea, a serious condition easily treated by a breathing machine.

Snoring can wreak havoc on a marriage if not addressed. Don't let it become a source of division in your marriage.

Snoring
Counselor's Commentary

Who imagines sleeping and snoring would be a cause for conflict? Of all the issues to find tools of coping, who would have thought it would be snoring?

Snoring is a common issue we don't see as something that would ruin a marriage. It's just a sleeping issue. An easy fix, right? Few people even mention it in premarital counseling. Nor is it discussed in most conversations as we ourselves contemplate marriage and our lives together. However, it is a significant factor and it is negatively impacting many marriages. Didn't think it was that serious, right? According to a 2013 study at UC Berkley "The Role of Sleep in Interpersonal Conflict: Do Sleepless Nights Mean Worse Fights?" by Amie Gordon and Serena Chen, approximately one third of all divorces are due to issues resulting from snoring. Who knew?

Sleep deprivation affects cognitive functioning and causes issues with memory, fatigue, and many other health problems. The spouse losing sleep sometimes finds the only way to actually get a full night's sleep is to leave their bed and go to the couch. Here is when the enemy gets a foot in the door. We understand we should have a feeling of togetherness, but many don't intentionally work to protect it. So when situations compromise it, we rarely feel it's a big interruption. We just think, "It's no big deal. I'll just sleep here because I'm irritable if I don't get sleep. It will make our relationship better."

But over time this arrangement starts to form a disconnect and eventually affects sexual and emotional intimacy. Some have resorted to sleeping in separate rooms for long periods. This has been a resolution some think has saved marriages and they have found a way to have feelings of togetherness. However, others feel going to bed separately, sleeping, and getting ready in the mornings has caused unresolved feelings of separation.

Usually the snorer misunderstands the magnitude of the impact on their mate, telling them to just "roll me over" or "tap me when it gets too loud" or "I don't snore that bad". The affected spouse becomes irritated and resentful and feels disregarded. Disregard leads to disappointment and sadness. If not addressed, it turns into anger and resentment displayed through passive aggressive actions.

Sleep deprivation from snoring and hearing it can lead to tension and cause conflict. Couples are less likely to successfully resolve conflict and show appreciation of their spouses. They approach each other with negativity and little patience.

As a result, issues many didn't think were a big deal have fatigued relationships. Spouses have reached outside of their marriage because a disconnection was caused by something that seemed harmless. Feelings of hopelessness have forced many to give up.

It's great that Michelle's prayer was answered by either his snoring stopped or her sleeping deepened to the point where she couldn't hear it. Many of us would love that ending; some would benefit from talking to a doctor. Many dealing with snoring feel as if there is no cure and few options. But there are and many do not lead to surgery. It is important to consult a physician who can give more information. Snoring can affect the health of the snorer as well as the one disturbed by snoring. This should be done together and in support of each other.

4 - Depressed Spouse

Couple: Jasmine and Aaron
Married: 8 years
Children: Aaron, Jr. (AJ) – age 6; Sydney – age 4

The Fourth of July picnic had gone fairly well. Aaron was, at least, physically present for the Bar-B-Q hosted at Jasmine's parents' home. Though he hadn't said much to anyone, he did sit with the family—her parents, brothers and their wives—at the tables while all of the kids played in the pool.

Their children had swum with their cousins for hours, diving into the water and having Styrofoam noodle fights. For once, their marriage seemed "normal" to Jasmine.

She noted the number of times the kids called to Aaron, "Hey dad! Look at this," and "Dad! Watch me." before performing some trick or another in the cool blue waterfall.

"Good job," Aaron acknowledged them, though his face retained its stillness as a result of the medication.

The kids are starving for his attention.

Following three hours at her parents' place, Jasmine, Aaron, and the kids went home. She supervised the kids' showers and changes of clothes while Aaron retreated to his office.

"Daddy looked really happy today," little Sydney remarked as Jasmine laid out a fresh set of clothes.

Jasmine blinked back tears. "Yes. He sure did, huh?"

"I wish he could be happy *every* day."

Jasmine also showered and changed from a blue maxi dress to a red tank top with white pants. Like the rest of America, she was in a celebratory mood.

Once she'd re-applied some of her makeup, she walked down the main hallway to Aaron's office and rapped on the door. "Babe. We need to get to the park so we can get a decent spot for fireworks."

Aaron kept one hand on the mouse. The other dangled off the arm of his executive chair. He didn't look up from the computer screen. "I'm really not up to it."

"What do you mean you're not *up to it*?"

"Exactly what I said."

She stepped completely into his office and shut the door behind her in hopes the kids wouldn't hear yet another argument. "Aaron, the kids are really looking forward to this."

Aaron sighed and finally looked up at his wife. "I can't."

"You *can* if you want to."

"I want to but I can't," Aaron insisted. "Today was…really hard for me. It took everything in me to get out for the time we were there. To put on a smile for you, your family, the kids,but I can't do it anymore. Besides, my head is killing me."

He winced as he began to rub his temples.

Jasmine wanted to feel sorry for him, but all her sympathy was spent on the kids at the moment. They didn't ask for a depressed dad who could only hold himself together for a few hours each day. "Aaron, it's only one day. We don't have another holiday until…what? September?"

Her husband covered his face with his hands. His voice boomed through the makeshift microphone. "You just don't get it. And I can't make you get it."

Jasmine let the tears fall this time. She shook her head. "You're right. I don't."

The kids asked questions, of course, during the dad-less ride to the city park.

"Why did Dad get sad again?" said AJ.

Sydney wanted to know, "Did *I* do something to make him sad?"

Jasmine glanced from the road momentarily to give Sydney a reassuring smile. "Oh no, honey. What's going on with Dad has nothing to do with you, me, or AJ"

Though they'd had this conversation several times over the past four months, their children's questions and insecurities about their father's condition never quite dissolved.

"Grandma said Dad's just crazy," AJ said.

"What?!"

"I heard her on the phone talking to Aunt Cathy. She said Dad needs to stop being selfish and snap out of it."

Jasmine bit her lip, literally, and took a deep breath. "You shouldn't listen to grown-ups on the phone, AJ That's called eavesdropping."

"Oh. Sorry."

"Anyway, Grandma loves your dad very much, but she is not a doctor. We're going to do what the doctors say, okay?"

"Yes, ma'am."

Jasmine wanted to call and fuss at her mother for voicing her opinion within earshot of a six-year-old. Not to mention the fact that she'd been discussing Aaron with Cathy. Yet, she could hardly argue with her mom's reasoning.

While Jasmine understood depression was a chemical imbalance, she also knew Aaron had thrown an enormous pity-party when he got laid off from his job the previous year. He'd moped around the house blaming everyone else for the pink slip. When Jasmine told him she didn't want to hear any more about it, he seemed to have withdrawn into himself. The silence only got worse when Aaron couldn't find a job after months of searching. He wanted to be left alone, wanted time to himself.

The man formed through this self-imposed isolation was nothing like the outgoing man she'd married. Nothing like the father AJ and Sydney had known only a year ago. This man—the one on medication, the one who slept fifteen hours a day, the one who wouldn't go see fireworks with his wife and kids—was *not* the man she'd married. Depression had stolen him and left her with someone she never would have even considered dating, let alone marrying.

Later that night, as the fireworks danced across the sky, she made a wish on one—as though it were a birthday cake candle. *God, please make my husband whole because I don't know how much longer I can do this.*

Depressed Spouse
Counselor's Commentary

"LORD! Of all the things people struggle with in a relationship. This is my battle?" So many have said this either out loud or way deep down in the crevices of their minds. "How and why am I dealing with this? What did I do to deserve this?"

Jasmine and Aaron have been married for eight years it's certain they've been through many difficult times. But this job loss for some reason or another has left a deep wound in her husband, their relationship, and their family.

Many women who are dealing with a depressed spouse may want to demand, "Man up already. Hurry and get better. Why can't you just snap out of it?"

Jasmine was aware of her husband's chemical imbalance, but she wanted her friend back. She understood how he felt and wanted the best for him. However, she wanted the husband she married and the father of her children to return to them. In some ways, she may have even felt abandoned and rejected. Questions of his commitment and love may begin to intrude upon her thoughts and convince her that he no longer loves her or their family.

As wives we may ask how and why does he have the luxury of checking out and I'm here to deal with life? Work, finances, kids, and family become solely one spouse's responsibility. All of it. This may lead to sadness, bitterness, resentment, and possibly anger. Expectations are not met and impatience begins to increase. There are some who even create situations to force their spouses to engage or become involved. Giving them tasks to complete, coercing their involvement in kid activities, obliging them to participate in family activities or dinner with friends are among the popular ones. If wives are not careful regarding their expectations in these situations, they may begin the process of disengaging from the husband and joining him in his depression. Depression knows no gender and does not discriminate in circumstance.

The number of men experiencing depression has increased because of the current economic instability and the experience of unemployment. That means many women have dealt with a depressed spouse. It does not mean it needs to overwhelm or destroy relationships and families.

There is hope. There are a few things one can do to navigate their way through this time.

As a support to the husband, they must first make sure they're taking care of themselves. Generally speaking, in marriage women thrive in making sure the relationship is intact and secure. We flourish when we feel heard, nurtured, and are given a sense of security. If not, on occasion we are apt to translate any sense of disconnection as our mission to analyze and resolve. As a result, we tend to assume responsibility for the thoughts and feelings of our spouses. We not only assume responsibility for their actions, we gravitate towards assuming their actions as a reflection of our ability to "wife." It is important that we keep a healthy distance from this internalizing as we support our husbands. Their responses and decisions are their responsibility. Although depression has a significant impact on one's ability to make healthy decisions, they continue to have a responsibility in their choices.

Also, we must not be governed by emotions and allow them to make our decisions during this time. It is a great idea to spend time with God and in His Word so that we can gain strength and direction. We cannot hear His voice if we don't know how He speaks. Unfortunately, when we react in emotions, we often end up saying or doing things in error and then regret. Our feelings get stirred up and drown out God's voice and His insight. We can possibly quit being a part of the supportive healing process and become confused in our purpose during this time. This may push us to say things that damage the husband and the relationship. Being driven by feelings will generate quick emotional decisions and consequently force us to live with life-long consequences.

In addition, it is so important to gather information and understand what our husband's situation involves. Get to know the signs and symptoms of depression.

According to the National Institute of Mental Health, the signs and symptoms of depression are:

- Feeling sad or "empty"
- Feeling hopeless, irritable, anxious, or angry

- Loss of interest in work, family, or once-pleasurable activities, including sex
- Feeling very tired
- Not being able to concentrate or remember details
- Not being able to sleep or sleeping too much
- Overeating, or not wanting to eat at all
- Thoughts of suicide, suicide attempts
- Aches or pains, headaches, cramps, or digestive problems
- Inability to meet the responsibilities of work, caring for family, or other important activities

Knowing this will give us strength in our efforts to provide support. It is important that we verbalize our love and acceptance for who he is and our willingness to uphold him as he struggles with these symptoms. As we become educated and verbalize our support, there is freedom in not assuming responsibility in the resolution.

In saying this, there is good news! You are not his counselor. Selah. Depression may be caused by a life event, but problems in other areas may exasperate the symptoms. You both can benefit from the expertise of a pastor or a licensed Christian counselor. This will relieve you from the self-imposed pressure of being the healer. You can seek help through Christian marital counseling. If your spouse refuses to participate, this may be your time to seek your own support through individual counseling. You can be equipped with healthy coping skills during this season of your life.

Lastly, take care of yourself. Eat healthy, exercise, get sleep, and pray often. Surround yourself with friends and family who might replenish what you feel depleted of as you maneuver during the difficult time. This is the reality of your life at this moment. It is what it is. No amount of fussing, cussing, kicking, and screaming can change this place. Accept this as your reality so both of you can begin the process of healing because things can get better.

5 - Emotionally Abusive Spouse

Couple: Pastor Chase and Deanne Remmy
Married: 9 years

"Let the church say...." Pastor Chase Remmy prompted.

"Amen," the congregation answered in unison.

Almost immediately, the hum of congregants bidding each other goodnight filled the small sanctuary. The Wednesday night crowd was a faithful bunch, so supportive of their new, younger pastor.

But his wife, Deanne, wondered if they would be as supportive if they knew what kind of man he was at home.

Deanne sat on the front pew, waiting and watching as Chase shook hands and traded hearty laughs with members who wished to congratulate him on another fine sermon or tell him about some restaurant they should try out in this small town.

She noticed the twinkle in his eyes as he entertained their conversation and gave them his full attention. This was all a part of his master plan to move up in the denomination. According to Chase, because he wasn't born into a powerful family, he'd have to pay his dues at a smaller church. But once they saw how good he was at managing and connecting with a "little nothing" congregation, they'd move him up. And up. And up.

These people were simply pawns in a game.

"Sister Deanne," one of the older women said in a whispery, sweet voice that caused Deanne to hoist up a fake smile. "You must be so proud of your husband."

"Yes, ma'am," she answered, careful to keep her eyes straight as she nodded. "I'm grateful."

Mother White, as the members called her, sat next to Deanne. "These old knees can't take too much standing."

Deanne smiled, genuinely this time.

Mother White was part of the unofficial welcoming committee at Main Street Church. She had to be in her mid-80's. Her husband was long gone, but her children visited church often—mostly to check on their mother, it seemed.

The older woman shook her head and leaned in closer to Deanne. "Now my deceased husband wasn't much of a church-goer. He was a good father and a good husband, but he was too nervous about coming to church."

"What was he afraid of?"

She gave a smug grin and shrugged her shoulders. "Oh, he had every excuse in the book. Came down to the fact that he just never felt good enough. He accepted Christ as his Savior, but he always felt like he fell short of living right, you know?"

Deanne nodded and patted Mother White's spotted hand. "Well, at least he was humble enough to know he needed a Savior." *And at least he wasn't pretending to be something he wasn't.*

The woman winked at Deanne. "That's why I like you and Pastor Remmy so much. Both of you are so positive. So kind. I thank God for sending you two here after Pastor Bud's death. You might even attract some of the younger people in this town."

"Thank you, Mother White."

Ten minutes and ten more congregants passed by, speaking to Chase and then offering a slight "hello" to Deanne. But she wasn't offended. It was her place to stay in the background, and she was quite content to do so.

After the sanctuary emptied, she and Chase stayed behind to lock the doors.

He was still having trouble trying to "jingle the key" as Deacon Maxwell had told him more than once.

In fact, Chase uttered a cuss word under his breath the third time he tried and failed to lock the doors.

Deanne looked around to make sure no one had heard her husband—the *real* Chase Remmy—slipping up.

"Let me try," she offered.

He shook his head. "As if." He gave it another go. This time it worked.

They began walking around the block toward their two-bedroom one-story house on First Street which had been provided by the church.

"I like the message you preached tonight."

"Thank you."

"Did you mean it? The part in Galatians five and twenty-two about the fruit of the Spirit?"

Chase sighed and walked faster.

Deanne sped up alongside him.

"Well?"

"Of course I meant it. The Holy Spirit changes us."

"So...what about *us?* Don't you think He wants *us* to be kind and patient with one another, too?"

Chase bristled. "Don't patronize me, Deanne. I'm doing my best to run a church, here. Your job is to *help* me—not *critique* me."

"All I'm saying is that it would be best if we both practiced what we preach," she tried to calm him, though the bulging vein at his temple told her she was already too late.

Chase pivoted and, suddenly, they were face-to-face.

"Stay in your lane," he warned.

Deanne swallowed hard.

"Pastor Remmy!" a voice called from behind them.

Instantly, Chase clasped Deanne's hand. His face softened.

Deanne pushed her cheeks high with a smile as they both turned to face the person.

It was Paul Maxwell, the good deacon's son. "My dad sent me to get the key from you. He's going to get another one made tomorrow."

"Great." Chase freed the difficult key from his ring and gave it to Paul. "Here you go."

"I'll take it to him right away."

"By the way," Chase smiled at the boy, "I hear you're filling out college applications. Can I pray for you?"

"Sure." The teenager bowed his head obediently.

Chase put both hands on the boy's shoulder and began to ask the Lord to give Paul favor and guidance in his life.

Deanne watched, wishing Paul would pray for her in this same gentle, loving tone.

When the prayer was over, Paul thanked Chase.

"Good night," Chase said.

"Night." Paul skipped away.

When the boy was out of sight, Paul released Deanne's hand.

Her smile fell.

They continued the trek.

As soon as they reached the house, Chase rushed to his office (formerly known as the second bedroom) and shut the door behind him.

Deanne rapped her knuckles on the door, not sure why she was even bothering. "You coming to bed soon?"

"No. I have to study for my next sermon."

Emotionally Abusive Spouse
Counselor's Commentary

What in the world is really going on here?

He's one way in public and completely different at home. Does he want to be married? Does he love his wife? Does he have a heart for the people of God?

Several women who've sought our counsel have tried to traverse the confusion of a husband they cannot figure out how to satisfy. The pull of their souls can be felt as they pour out the longing in their hearts. They're reaching and grasping at the dream of living out the picture they've been painting for years—the happily-ever-after masterpiece. But it's not working.

If most of us were honest, we got married looking beyond who our spouses were and lived for the person they would become. We fell in love with this person who hadn't arrived yet. There is great potential. We've seen glimpses of him. So we wait. We wait for the change.

While we wait, we try our best to be the woman for *that* man. We've seen him. It was great. At the beginning, it was a whirlwind. We laughed. We enjoyed our time together. He was the man of our dreams, left nothing to the imagination, and he knew exactly what to say and do.

But now, things have changed. He's no longer here. The honeymoon is over. In this case, Deanne is wondering how to be let back in.

Who is this person I've committed the rest of my life to? What happened? I thought I knew him.

Is this what she's dealing with?

Deanne knew that her husband's focus wasn't on her. He had a dream that only included her presence, but not her involvement. But she waited. She played the role that was handed to her.

She didn't believe this was the person she'd married. *He* would return if she waited.

Listen to her inward conversations:

We were great when we got together. It can be like that again. If I could just wait a little longer. If I could just say the right word or find the right scripture that would change how he feels about me. If I could be patient and do the work for him, then it will get better. If I could fix the things about me that irritate him, then he will want to be with me. If I could just be a better wife, then he will include me in his dream. If I could just lose weight, then he would be proud to be with me. If I could just wait a little longer, he will see what a great wife I am.

Unfortunately for Deanne, none of these will fix her marriage or change the way her husband feels about her.

Why? Her thoughtfulness, weight loss, patience, waiting, or changing are not a remedy to his character.

Their marriage is built on the moods and behaviors of Chase and has thus become toxic in nature. Toxic marriages are built on the moods or behaviors of one person. Healthy relationships are built on a foundation of love, shared respect, free will, and common goals.

Toxic or bad marriages have these signs:

- Controlling spouse
- Lack of intimacy
- Blame
- Emotional abuse (name calling, ridicule, withholding affection)
- Emotional Withdrawal
- Living together, but separate in daily lives
- Oneness is not the goal of the relationship
- Lack of respect
- Different or confusing behaviors in front of others

Because toxic relationships or bad marriages have no visible scars, we often treat them as something we can fix. So instead, we become a participant in the cycle. We work within it trying to get back to the person we once knew. Or we participate as we try to reach the person they can become.

One major problem in the Remmy's marriage is that Deanne's behaviors help maintain the toxic tendencies of her husband. She takes on the role and tries her best to make sure that others are not aware. As part of the cover-up, she participates in the toxic relationship, yet tries to change it at the same time. This usually results in assuming the sole responsibility for changing his behavior. Most likely she'll be left with feelings of confusion, helplessness, lack of self-worth, and feelings of failure.

At this point, it's best that, along with prayer, she reach out for professional help. Another perspective can help her find clarity on her role and expectations of her husband. As she seeks help, she should ask but not expect the participation of her husband. It is important the goal of obtaining help be about her well-being and not another attempt to find ways for changing his behavior.

Not being an emotional participant is important. Ridding herself of the "if only" and thriving despite his moods or behaviors is critical in gaining perspective and strength. It takes two individuals to maintain a toxic relationship. The perpetrator and the participant. Once strength is introduced, it usually facilitates change in the trajectory of the relationship. Strength is not yelling or demanding change. It's her responding out of truth, not accepting responsibility for his behavior, and choosing to care for her own emotional health. There is no guarantee the perpetrator will change. However, it will establish precedence for changed responses from both that may eventually bring about a constructive change in behavior. This can lead to progress in themselves as well as their marriage. Unfortunately, some differences in the participant's responses may escalate anger and threats of harm from the perpetrator, sensing a threat to their control.

Note: This is not applicable to situations of physical abuse. Emotionally toxic relationships often progress into physical abuse. If this is the situation, help and a safer environment should be sought immediately by contacting the local authorities, family and friends.

6 - The "Get Over It" Chapter

With a combined forty plus years of marriage between the Stimpsons and the Riddicks, Shundria and I knew there was a limitless supply of "little things" that bug us—and our spouses—for which we could write many chapters. However, there's a limit to the number of pages that can be printed in a book per the publishers.

That said, we thought it would be interesting to list and ask our husbands to list a number of things that we've had to simply build a bridge and "get over." There has been no resolution other than for the offended party to make the decision to stop *taking* offense. In other words, with time, we've learned that these things are not even worth arguing about anymore. With the exception of an occasional flare-up, we *don't* talk even about them anymore. We're not upset about them and don't treat our spouses differently when they occur. God was never angry about them in the first place. They're just the quirks that create the beautifully unique tapestry of our individual marriages.

The Riddicks
Chris has gotten over Shundria's
- PMS moods

- Despising the laundry (He does it for me! Bless Jesus!)
- Talking to him about everything while he's watching his TV shows or movies
- Constantly misplacing the cell phone
- Leaving hair pins and pony tail holders all over the house
- Using his deodorant (works better than mine)
- Always wanting to try something new

Shundria has gotten over Chris's
- Leaving his shoes where he took them off
- TV/movie bingeing
- "All you have to do is" response to dilemmas
- Not wanting to go to social gatherings ("I don't know them")
- Using the countertops as a shelf to put anything and everything on top
- Not wanting to try new things (doesn't like change)

The Stimpsons

Stevie has gotten over Michelle's
- Terrible cooking (I tried. It's just not my gift. Stevie agrees.)
- Wearing his black socks
- Moving stuff and not putting it back in the original spot
- Leaving on lights in unoccupied rooms
- Batch cleaning method (I clean up when it's getting kinda bad around here)

- Tendency to be overly dramatic about the kids
- Telling long stories
- Habit of leaving half-empty water bottles all over the house

Michelle has gotten over Stevie's
- Sighing in a condescending manner
- Answering a question with a question (i.e. Q: "What time is it?" A: "Where's your watch?")
- Sleeping with the TV on
- Fussy zones (sleepy, tired, hungry, stressed— usually later in the workweek)
- Frank personality

So here's the million-dollar question
How did you GET OVER IT?

Michelle: I think my first step in getting over the little stuff was to remember how many "little things" I must do every day that God overlooks in love because He knows I'm ignorant, afraid, or just acting like a spiritual baby. His love and mercy provide the basis.

Beyond this, one thing that I have learned to do is to stop taking everything my husband does or says personally. For example, if my husband is in a fussy mood, that has nothing to do with me. He has made the decision to be fussy in that moment. It's a free world. He has every right to decide to be fussy. I'm also a free person, and I can choose not to match his mood because, hey, I'm me! 1 fussy person + 0 fussy person = 1 fussy person. It's not mandatory that I add to the drama. Ironically, I think the best model for this has been my husband. When I get dramatic, he intentionally turns his attitude down a notch to balance me out. He really is a peacemaker...unless he's tired or hungry. LOL!

Shundria: My light bulb moment was realizing that he has an experience in the marriage as well. I wasn't the only one annoyed. So, I imagined how it would feel to be married to me. Consequently, I began to think about my moods, anger, and many feelings. It became easier for me to extend grace because I so desperately needed it. I've been so freely loved and forgiven by a Perfect Savior. How can I, being so full of inconsistencies, not extend the same?

A significant turning point was when I understood and accepted that we are not the same. We do not have to do things the exact same way or agree on everything. It was a relief to cancel the goal of being validated only when he agreed with my perception. I stopped holding him responsible for my feelings and myself for his. Embracing the differences and respecting them have allowed for deeper connection.

Now you've taken a peek inside *our* marriages. We pray that our transparency and imperfections will hasten you to the point where you realize that you may be ruminating, thereby allowing tiny seeds of bitterness to be planted. Those seeds, watered and nourished by bickering, eventually become weeds with the potential to choke the very life from your marriage. Kill them with love. Forgive quickly. Time yourself if you have to and break your forgiveness-time record with each opportunity. Before you know it, you'll come to a point where you realize it was never worth getting upset in the first place.

7 – The Passive-Aggressive Spouse

Couple: Donald and Rochelle
Married: 10 years
Children: Tyler – age 8; Elizabeth – age 6; DJ – age 5

"Don't forget. We're going to visit my mother tomorrow," Rochelle reminded Donald as she turned off the lamp. She snuggled under the covers. "Did you hear me?"

"I have ears."

"Okay, I'll wake you up at eight."

"Yes, mother dear," Donald teased.

Rochelle checked the digital clock again to make sure the alarm was set correctly. They needed to be on the road by nine to make it to the assisted living facility by ten o'clock. She wanted to arrive between breakfast and lunch so she wouldn't take her mother out of her routine. Rochelle's sister, Laronique, had reiterated how important it was to keep their mother on a routine now that she was in a different stage of Alzheimer's.

"Don't be upset if she doesn't recognize you, the kids, and Donald right away. Don't take it personal—it's the disease."

"Okay." Rochelle had promised her older sister, but wasn't sure how she'd react if her own mother didn't remember her. She could understand if Mom didn't recognize Donald; they'd only been married ten years. And kids change as they grow. Not remembering them was understandable. *But me?* Rochelle didn't want to freak out or have a meltdown, which was precisely why she wanted Donald there—for support. Granted, he was no psychologist, but he'd at least be a shoulder to lean on.

The next morning, when the alarm went off, Rochelle slammed it and shook Donald's shoulder. "Up, up, up."

He didn't move. He had never been a morning person.

She brushed her teeth and washed her face, then went back to their bed. This time, she shook him until he opened his eyes. "I'll get the kids ready. You can go ahead and get in the shower."

Twenty minutes later, Rochelle had the kids up and ninety percent dressed. She'd toasted the frozen waffles, warmed the turkey bacon on the grill, put the food on the kids' plates, and poured their glasses of orange juice. They would eat while she dressed.

But when she crossed the living room back to the master bedroom, she opened the door and found Donald still asleep in bed. "What in the world are you doing? We're leaving in thirty minutes."

He raised up and glanced at the alarm clock, then collapsed back on the bed, mumbling, "I'm so sorry, babe. I'll go next time."

"No. You're going *this* time. We've still got half an hour before we get on the road. Come on. Get up so we can go."

He remained still. "I'm really tired."

"Are you kidding me?" Rochelle huffed, her hands suddenly drawn to her hips. She wanted to snatch the covers right off his body and douse a bucket of cold water on Donald's back.

Slowly, he crawled out of bed and stomped off to the bathroom.

Satisfied that her husband was indeed on the go, Rochelle grabbed a shirt and a pair of linen pants from her closet. Both pieces of clothing needed a bit of ironing, so she dashed back through the kitchen to check on the kids, then on to the laundry room to take care of the wrinkles.

While ironing, she heard the shower running. *Thank God.* Donald was getting ready. But with him getting into the shower so late, there wouldn't be enough hot water for her to take a shower before the trip. She'd have to wing it on last night's shower and catch up when she got back.

That settled in her mind, Rochelle grabbed a sports bra from the never-ending pile of clean unfolded clothes. She dressed herself right there in the laundry room.

Emerging, she looked in on the kids once more. "DJ, finish your meat," she said, passing through.

We're gonna make it on time.

She had planned to talk to the kids on the way about their grandmother's diminished mental capacity; she wanted to prepare them for the worst. And she was counting on Donald's calm, cool state of mind to buffer the bad news with a distraction or humor. Both she and the kids needed him today.

Yet, when she entered their room, she found him sitting on the bed in his underwear, watching ESPN.

"Dude! What are you doing? We've got less than fifteen minutes until we get out of here."

He stuck a finger in his ear, apparently trying to unclog water. "I'm getting ready, ain't I?"

"Yes, but you're taking *forever*. You wasted time when you didn't get up, and now here you are watching television."

He sighed. "Why don't I just stay home?"

"No. That's not the plan."

"The way you're acting, I don't even want to go."

Rochelle took a deep breath. "Donald. We've been talking about this for weeks now. I finally have a Saturday off, which does *not* happen at this time of year with my job. We *planned* to use this day to visit my mother."

"I know. I'm just saying. I'm trying to get ready, but all you're doing is fussing."

"Fine. I'll leave you alone. But we need to be ready by nine. Period."

Rochelle dusted her face with powder, threw her hair into a ponytail, donned a pair of earrings, threw on a pair of Sperrys and pronounced herself "ready" to Donald, who had only made it as far as putting on a pair of shorts.

She finished the last ten percent of kid-preparation. Then she and the kids sat in the living room.

"What are we waiting for?" Elizabeth asked, her feet impatiently dancing over the ledge of couch cushioning.

"Daddy," Rochelle answered. She turned on the television. "We're waiting for Daddy."

And wait they did. Nine o'clock came. Ten after nine came.

"What's taking him so long?" DJ wanted to know.

"I don't know. Tyler, go tell your father that we're all ready to leave now."

Her oldest child obeyed immediately and returned with an announcement. "Daddy says we can go without him."

Rochelle popped off the couch and rushed to their bedroom. "Donald. We're already behind schedule. Let's go."

"I haven't had breakfast. And you know I can't take my medicine on an empty stomach. You and the kids might as well go because I still have to eat."

"You're just making excuses."

"You want *me* to get sick, too?" he yelled back.

"I don't *care* if you get sick! Let's get out of here."

"That's it! I'm not going." He pulled the shirt over his back probably ten times quicker than he'd put it on.

Rochelle could only manage a cynical chuckle. "That's all you wanted in the first place. To stay home. Why can't you just be a man and say it?"

"I *was* going. *You* ruined it."

"Yeah, right."

Rochelle left the room, slamming the door behind her. She and the kids would go it alone. Rochelle decided to put up a wall to protect herself from feeling too much because she didn't want the kids to see her having a breakdown.

She'd have to deal with her real emotions later.

Passive-Aggressive Spouse
Counselor's Commentary

Does this scenario sound familiar to you? My father used to say, "Say what you mean and mean what you say!" This is one of those instances where this bit of advice could have been useful for Donald and Rochelle. At the point of sleeping in late, somebody should have started a discussion about what was really going on.

Aggressive feelings being demonstrated in passive ways is known as passive-aggressive. The most difficult behaviors to deal with in a marriage, they are confusing, difficult to determine, and understated. The couple is usually in the storm of a conflict before they've had a chance to identify they're even dealing with them.

Usually, the passive-aggressive party hasn't developed constructive ways to address their anger. They learned earlier in their lives that the expression of anger is unacceptable. Therefore, they outwardly appear to be cooperative and caring. But behaviorally they are angry, spiteful and retaliatory. They do not respond overtly when they are upset, but they will disrupt any attempt to resolve an issue.

One behavior in particular that is frequently found in these relationships is withdrawing. The passive-aggressive will recede during a dispute with a "whatever" and leave the other party feeling responsible for their behavior and for fixing the situation. They take most confrontations as a personal attack and their goal is to extract revenge. Often they lack insight and resort to blaming anyone except themselves for their behavior or retreat.

In the case of Donald and Rochelle, he knew the night before he didn't want to go to the facility. However, instead of verbalizing this decision and perhaps his fears, he agreed. He sabotaged her morning, blamed her, and eventually decided to withdraw. This response and skewed view of reality allowed him to reach the intended goal of not going.

Other signs worth noting are:

- Not following through on promises or agreements
- Blaming others for their failures
- The silent treatment
- Sullenness
- Procrastination
- Sabotaging
- Complaining

Dealing with this behavior takes patience and the ability to be direct. It's important to discuss how their behaviors are affecting others—not merely the behaviors. If only their behaviors are discussed, they may immediately shut down and refuse to participate in anything constructive. If this happens, at a minimum, you were able to voice your feelings.

It's also beneficial to stay on subject and only discuss the facts. The discussion should have a time limit and be goal-oriented. Many times in these relationships, the subject is changed and the argument becomes about the target spouse, as opposed to the impact of the passive-aggressive behavior. This action often leaves the target feeling frustrated as if they are the cause for the problems in the relationship.

A word of caution: Sometimes demands that other's needs be met and setting deadlines often fuel the fire of this behavior. It gives more reason for the passive-aggressive to withdraw or withhold and not meet the need. Recognize that when one has asked and find they're repeating their request, as Rochelle repeatedly asked Donald to wake up and hurry, they are already in the cycle of the destructive behavior. Donald knew the importance of the visit with her mother and was also aware of the time. Rochelle could have verbalized how his procrastination was causing her to feel unsupported and continued with her plans. As he continued to delay, this was an indicator for her to step away from the conflict and refuse to join in the cycle. Continuing her request resulted in him accusing her of fussing and giving him an excuse to withdraw. Instead of taking the bait, one should acknowledge their own feelings of anger and refuse to participate.

There is hope that the more the effects of the behavior are acknowledged, it will eventually become evident that there is need for change. Not addressing or acknowledging this destructive behavior will only reinforce it. Unaddressed passive-aggressive behaviors can destroy relationships.

It is essential not to internalize this cycle. As in most instances the origin of these behaviors preceded the relationship. Make it a goal to create a supportive, loving, atmosphere that facilitates discussions about fear, resentment, and anger.

8 - Communication Problems Galore

Couple: Javier and Patricia Hernandez
Married: 24 years
Children: Cecelia and Daniel, both in college

Outside Javier was blowing the horn, which slightly irritated Patricia. Their son Daniel's college was only an hour and a half away. They'd make it to the Honor Society induction with time to spare. Daniel had already said he couldn't visit with them until after the ceremony. She didn't appreciate Javier rushing her for no reason.

Which earrings should I wear? She fished through her jewelry box and held up a gold hoop near her left ear and a bronze cross near her right.

Hoops.

Then Patricia dabbed on another coat of lipstick and, although she was ready, decided to get a few bottles of water for the trip. She checked herself in the mirror one last time. After nearly starving herself for a week so that she could look good in front of the other moms at the college, she was able to fit into her size 10 all-occasion black dress. Not bad for a forty-something-year-old mother of two.

The horn blew again.

Okay, now he's really pushing it. Patricia grabbed her wedge sandals while sliding her traveling slippers onto her feet. She stomped out of the house and got into the car with Javier.

"Aye! What were you doing in there?"

She had barely closed the door when he took off in reverse.

"Getting ready."

"It's not that serious."

She strapped on her seatbelt. "Yes it is. We're honoring Danny today."

Javier shook his head, putting the car in Drive and speeding down their street as though he was being pursued.

"We're going to make it on time," Patricia sighed.

Javier turned up the music and some rap artist—*Jay Z? Lil' Wayne?*—somebody they were both too old to be listening to blared through the speakers. Patricia took her iPod and headphones from her purse and tried to override the vulgarities with an old playlist full of Christian music by Joann Rosario and Jaci Velasquez.

Just as she'd predicted, they arrived forty minutes before they needed to be there. As Javier pulled into the parking space at the student center, Patricia texted their son: *We're here.*

He replied: *I'll text you when they open the doors.*

Patricia paraphrased the message. "Danny says we're too early. Doors aren't open yet."

Javier didn't say anything. He just stopped the car and rolled the windows down.

There was no way her husband would admit she was right. But she'd settle for the fact that they both knew he'd been wrong.

She decided not to rub it in anymore. After all, the songs she'd just listened to reminded her about forgiveness, love, and gratitude. She had much to be thankful for. Both of her children were in college—Danny a freshman and Cecelia a junior at a major university. Everyone was healthy. She and Javier had both recently been promoted at their jobs, and now that they were finally empty-nesters, they could sit back and enjoy life. Maybe even make more trips to Mexico to visit family.

Days like this one were supposed to be the icing on the cake, the reward for sticking together through hard times and making sacrifices to raise great kids in a crazy society.

Thank you, God, for a great life.

Twenty minutes later, several more families had arrived and parked. Patricia watched as an older couple, presumably grandparents, walked slowly up the stairs of the small building and opened the door.

"Thought you said the doors were locked," Javier said, pointing toward the entrance.

Just then, a female wearing a plain white maxi dress and flip-flops stepped out of the building and motioned to let the growing crowd know that building was open.

"They were, obviously," Patricia vindicated herself.

Dozens of car doors opened as the proud family members exited vehicles. Patricia changed shoes before stepping out and quickly noticed that none of the other women were dressed quite as professionally. In fact, some wore jeans and t-shirts.

"Looks like you spent all that time getting dressed up for nothing," Javier mumbled under his breath as they walked toward the building.

"I'd rather be overdressed than underdressed." She flipped her long brown locks behind her shoulder.

"Whatever. It's not like you're a fashion model."

Patricia stopped. "What's that supposed to mean?"

"Exactly what I said. You're *not* a fashion model. You're a regular person."

"A regular person?"

"Yes."

"So I'm nothing special to you? All that I do for you, to look good, to contribute to this family?"

Javier looked toward the sky.

Patricia stepped closer to him to let another couple go by. "I mean *nothing* to you?"

"Stop putting words in my mouth."

"Hmph." *You won't have to worry about words coming from me for a long time.*

The ceremony was quick and to the point. Faculty members read the purpose of the organization and an alumni member gave a short speech about the importance of always doing your best. The new inductees to the Honor Society were named, given a special lapel pen, and arranged to shake hands and take pictures with the dean.

Patricia sat next to Javier, but didn't say a word.

At the reception, which took place in the hallway just outside the small auditorium, Patricia's countenance instantly shifted when she saw Danny. She gave him a big hug and a once-over to make sure he'd been eating well in the past few months.

Javier congratulated their son as well.

"Thanks, Dad. But I'm starving for some *real* food. Can we go out to eat?"

At the restaurant, Patricia was careful to keep the conversation focused on Danny. She laughed, asked and answered his questions. She even commented on things Javier said to Danny, but said nothing directly to Javier.

It wasn't until they got in the car and Javier asked, "Have you gotten his books yet?" that the game was officially on.

"Hello?" he said to her.

Patricia snapped the buckle and changed shoes again.

"I'm talking to you."

He'd started the car but was still parked, waiting for an answer.

Patricia slowly turned her head toward him and gave him a glare so sharp it could have slashed four tires.

Javier's face twisted in confusion "What?"

Patricia squinted her eyes more. "Really?"

He shrugged. "Really *what*?"

****

That was two days ago.

Patricia hadn't uttered a word to Javier since then. She wasn't even responding to texts or email messages unless they pertained to household matters.

As childish as this silent treatment was, there was nothing Javier could do about it until his wife snapped out of her fit.

Communication Problems Galore
Counselor's Commentary

After twenty-four years of marriage, one would think that Javier and Patricia would have learned the art of effective communication. Beginning with the honk of the horn to the squinting of the eyes, this couple isn't talking, but they are screaming they're frustrated with each other. It's so unfortunate that we can exist for years in a relationship and never develop skills to effectively communicate our deepest thoughts and desires.

There are two parts to communication, listening and talking. Most of us talk and then we wait to talk. It is rare that we actually listen to what our spouses are saying to us. We hear the words, but don't listen to the feelings. In most cases we are having two different conversations. Each person listens through different filters. Here, the term filter describes what is used to provide perspective and understanding in communication. Childhood, faith, life experiences, failure, success, family of origin, unhealthy advice or teaching, past relationships, learned behavior, age, etc., are all part of our filters.

When we communicate, we use these filters to discriminate information and form a response. Sadly, they're not often saturated in the Word of God but are drenched in our own definitions and opinions. Eventually, we use this faulty information to make decisions in our relationships. It is amazing that we never question how we formed our "rules" that make such critical decisions. We rarely seek to replace this misinformation with the truth of God's Word.

Javier commented to Patricia that she overdressed and was not a supermodel. Regardless of his intent, she heard she was not special and meant nothing to him. This was an argument that began when he honked the horn. Every action until her decision to give him the silent treatment supported her feelings of not being valued or special. She even made sure she defined her value by making it obvious that she was correct regarding the time of the ceremony.

Although Javier used few words, he ensured they communicated his frustrations. His wife may not have taken the statement as he intended, but his timing and context were neither supportive or constructive. Both were indicating they were hurt and frustrated for different reasons. Instead of discussing these feelings, they chose to use faulty information to aim their words and actions as weapons to seek revenge. After twenty-four years of practice, they had mastered this process.

Using faulty information can facilitate misunderstandings and false accusations that can also lead us to behave destructively as in the actions of Patricia. Many of us tend to use the silent treatment as a means of demanding that our needs be met. Our goal is to communicate the lack of value or respect for the other party. The silence intentionally conveys their very presence doesn't matter enough to even acknowledge. This leaves our spouse feeling insignificant, isolated, rejected, and guilty.

As the silent party, we often hold the power and tend to control the emotional atmosphere in the relationship. We can direct conversation away from having to confront our feelings of rejection or camouflage our lack of tools to handle difficult issues. This shutdown is a way to excuse us from functioning and force our partner to cave in and meet our demands. This is emotional bullying. It causes deep emotional scarring that builds walls and eliminates the environment that fosters growth and intimacy. It's also labeled as a form of emotional abuse.

In some instances, our excuse in using this calculated silence is to imply that we'd rather not talk than to say something hurtful. I agree that we must bridle our tongues as we are instructed in Proverb 21:24, "Whoever keeps his mouth and his tongue, keeps himself out of trouble." However, the alternative is not verbal lashing and abuse. Neither is constructive or nurtures relationships. It's the same as asking, "What causes the most pain—being hit by a bus or train?" They both hurt.

Dealing with the silent treatment in the relationship involves healthy, effective communication. Initially it is important that one grasps an understanding of the reasons for their spouse's treatment. We cannot help in solving a problem we don't know exists. Assuming one can fix the problem on their own is an irrational expectation. Both should be involved. This can be done when both are ready and willing to have a productive conversation. Begging or forcing dialogue may empower the partner, resulting in even longer silence. The ignored mate must wait until the other is ready, going through their days as normal as possible without contributing to an atmosphere of conflict.

This is not to say that the silent treatment be used as a response either. It means that you do not participate in this struggle for emotional power. Issues can only be addressed when the climate is calmed, emotions are stable, and both are capable of having a beneficial dialogue.

Sometimes you have to be the first to break the silence. Some partners need the prompting of the other to help get out of their sullenness. It does not seem fair or right. However, neither fair nor right can be used to gauge healthy relationships, only righteousness can. Your willingness to approach can begin the process of healing. Let them know that how they feel is important and you care about what they are experiencing. This is a form of humility. This can facilitate productive communication resulting in connectedness and greater intimacy.

At the core of any relationship, we want to be valued and loved. We put ourselves in positions of vulnerability and transparency in order to receive them from our spouse. At the point of any hurt or rejection, we tend to fiercely protect our hearts and chase a false sense of security that disguises itself as power and control. Thus resulting in unhealthy tools of communication that only push us further away from our deepest desires of support and togetherness.

It takes time to re-route the patterns after decades of poor communication, but it can be done. Even if only one partner is willing to change initially, the impact of that decision can be far-reaching, especially when combined with prayer. If unsure of how to even start the wheels of change, it's best to involve a therapist who can provide the missing tools.

9 - Husband Won't Keep a Job

Couple: London and Olivia Christopher
Married: 4 years

After a brief, professional introduction, Olivia unwound the string between the two round fasteners, opening the envelope containing their W-2 forms, mortgage tax statement, student loan interest record, and donation receipts. She slid the short stack of papers onto the accountant's desk.

"Here's our stuff." Olivia sighed casually.

The accountant, Sean, had been recommended by one of Olivia's co-workers. Sean gave a slight grunt as he eyed the papers. "You guys must have lots of investments?"

"No." Olivia shook her head.

"Properties?"

"No." Olivia realized then that Sean had obviously mistaken her for a financially well-to-do client.

Sean sifted through the documents. "Oh. I see now."

Olivia blushed with embarrassment. Of the twenty or so papers in the stack, roughly half of them were from her husband, London's, short-lived jobs. Three hundred dollars here, twelve hundred dollars there. Nothing more than a few thousand because as soon as London got jobs, he managed to lose them.

Sean cleared his throat. "Did you complete the online information request?"

"Yes," Olivia said with a nod.

"Looks like I have all we need. I'll see you Friday at one to finish up?"

"Yes. Thank you."

Olivia stood and quickly exited the door of the small office. Blinking back tears, she got into her BMW and started the engine. Sean's reaction to the number of London's W-2s only confirmed Olivia's most heinous thoughts about her husband. He was a lazy, undisciplined good-for-nothing loser-mooch who had gone from his mother's purse strings to Olivia's with the simple phrase "I do."

Olivia drove from the business park wondering and crying out to God, "How could I have missed this? How did I end up marrying someone who can't keep a job? God, what did I miss?"

With her mind on autopilot as she traveled from this familiar part of town toward home, she skittered through memories of their courtship.

Perhaps she should have known things weren't quite right when they moved in together. They'd decided Olivia would pay the rent, their largest bill, because she was paid monthly by the school district in a lump sum. At the time, it just made sense. She also took care of the payments on her BMW.

London was to pay the smaller bills as they came in, since he was paid weekly.

Things went well for the first few months, but London started missing electricity and cell phone payments somewhere around the third month.

"Babe, this envelope is *pink.*" She had confronted him when the energy company's bill arrived overdue the first time.

"Man!" London had grabbed the envelope from her before she could open it. "They're crazy. I paid that bill. I'll call them tomorrow and get it straightened out."

Since the lights never went off, Olivia assumed London had been telling the truth. But when his sister, Roxanne, mentioned to Olivia weeks later at a family birthday party that London needed to "stop asking Momma for money to pay his bills." Olivia had been dumbstruck.

Later, she'd confronted London, who said he'd handle his sister and her *lying* mouth.

Yep. That should have been my first clue.

But she'd been too in love with London to see the signs. Not only that, the truth was London *did* work back then. He might not have had steady work, but if push came to shove, he'd pull out his clippers and spend a weekend at his friend's barbershop taking the walk-ins to make extra cash.

Olivia admired the "hustle" in London. It made her feel like no matter what, she'd have someone in her corner. Someone who would do anything to make things happen.

All that changed after they got married.

Olivia quickly received two promotions with the school district, from a campus instructional coach to the central office curriculum team, nearly doubling her income. With that increase came London's decrease in the desire to contribute steadily.

They'd gone to counseling, where Olivia learned that London felt he was "unnecessary" in her life because she didn't need him financially. Sitting on that couch with London last year, Olivia wondered what happened to the man who used to be out the door before the sun rose? What happened to hustle-man?

"Babe, I love *you*," she had pleaded with him. "This isn't even about money."

"For now, just listen." The counselor had reminded Olivia.

"It's like this," London explained, "when I try to do stuff, she's already taken care of it. We had a plumbing situation in the guest bathroom. I had a friend who was going to come over Saturday to fix it, but Olivia had already talked to our builder—"

"That's because the house is still under warranty. It makes no sense to pay for something that might be covered."

"Mrs. Christopher," the counselor prompted Olivia to close her mouth again.

Olivia took a deep breath and tried to listen, but it was impossible. How could she sit there and listen to accusations about herself that were, basically, excuses for why London wouldn't or couldn't keep a job?

After London finished his spiel, the counselor asked Olivia to rephrase London's concerns.

"He feels like I don't need him, so he's not going to get a job," Olivia blurted out.

"That's *not* what I said. Don't put words in my mouth."

"That's the *truth* without the pretty excuse-paint on it."

Needless to say, the counseling hadn't done the trick. Olivia was still working herself to death while London had the luxury of working whenever he felt like it and quitting when his boss required more of him or someone wrote him up for being late. If Olivia made a big enough stink about things, London would "borrow" some money from his mother.

The only good decision Olivia could say she'd made thus far with regard to London was that they hadn't had any kids. Bringing a child into this mess would only double the chaos. Olivia had made up in her mind that if London didn't get his act together soon, they wouldn't be having any kids or any marriage.

The tax preparer's incorrect assumption only strengthened her resolve. Either London got a steady job or Olivia was out of there.

Husband Won't Keep a Job
Counselor's Commentary

How did Olivia and London get together? How did Olivia decide London was dependable? Why did the "hustle-man" in London not anticipate the expectation of stability from Olivia? It is not at all surprising that Olivia is contemplating divorce and London is feeling inadequate.

Although we say we accept our spouses as they are, it is more accurate to say we accept them now until we convince them to change later. We have both spoken and unspoken expectations and sometimes hold our spouses to the expectations of our own needs instead of the responsibilities of our God-given roles. Our expectations of each other and ourselves must be filtered through God's Word. Ephesians 5:22-33 and Titus 2:4 provide the framework of a loving relationship.

Some of what we're expecting from our spouses can only be fulfilled by our Savior. Resolving our past issues or meeting all of our emotional needs are not the responsibility of a spouse—neither is parenting and monitoring our behavior.

It is important we accept full responsibility for the choice of our own behaviors. We often inadequately address issues. Rather we blame the other for what we deem their lack of success in not meeting all of our needs. Rarely do we discuss our expectations constructively or look for ways to best care for each other and our relationship. Our expectations are to be on the receiving end of the love described in I Corinthians 13. However, we don't interpret these scriptures as what we should *give*.

In the case of Olivia and London, let's first consider the influence of their own needs and how they affect their personal expectations and perception. Feelings of neglect and disappointment altered their treatment of each other.

Olivia's perception of London was distorted by her feelings of love and infatuation. She labeled his actions through her own ideals of what a relationship should be. As a result, she mistakenly defined London's "hustling" as a sentiment to be productive instead of a reluctance to maintain reliable employment or income and build wealth. The fact that London was often in "hustle" mode was a clear indication he was accustomed to functioning in crisis mode. Absent a crisis (which he does not have since Olivia will pay all the bills), London has trouble finding motivation to work.

Consequently, their financial issues have caused Olivia to change her perception of London's actions. Hustling has now become irresponsible and lazy, no longer an endearing quality. She's expecting behaviors that he has yet to demonstrate. Olivia's reality is that London is not in a position to contribute to her expectation of leadership and trustworthiness in his role as husband. As a result, she is experiencing feelings of betrayal, abandonment, and helplessness.

London's viewpoint of Olivia is changing as well. He believed that her approval of his "hustling" was a validation regarding his way of providing. London may have "mom" expectations of Olivia, wanting her to be an enabler of his behavior without interrogation or protest. Questioning his decisions or behavior may contribute to his feelings of inadequacy. To avoid these confrontations, he has been dishonest. London has violated trust in this relationship by lying about his financial struggles due to the shame associated with not being able to meet the expectations. He has manipulated circumstances and others to avoid the consequences of his immaturity. London is now realizing the impact of his behavior associated with his poor decision-making. This has led to distrust and distance from Olivia. Although he may struggle with feelings of insignificance, it does not abdicate his responsibility of honesty and financial contribution.

The issue in some marriages is what may have worked financially or behaviorally as a single person does not work as a partner in a relationship. This lack of regard for the outcome of financial irresponsibility has contributed to building resentment, distrust, and anger in marriages. Blaming Olivia for her inattentiveness to behaviors before marriage and London's lack of financial contribution and honesty would be easy and correct. Unfortunately many marriages stop at identifying the blame, but rarely do we honestly accept our contribution and offer solutions.

There are a few steps that can be taken to help Olivia and London reach resolution and not separation.

Communication is extremely important in establishing realistic expectations within this relationship and financial situation. Avoiding money talks only makes matters worse.

They have to examine the vulnerability within their relationship and discuss the gravity of their financial situation. By exploring and questioning their own expectations, they open doors to allow discussions of personal responsibility and acceptance.

The collaboration's intent is to develop financial goals and assign roles in meeting them—not to place blame. Both can discuss how each can contribute and remain honest as they work towards meeting their goals. Goals should be attainable, but within the potential of each spouse. Regular meetings may help maintain accountability. Open and frank discussions regarding finances can be supportive, build trust, and establish deeper intimacy.

In addressing what is true, Olivia and London have an opportunity to care for each other and their relationship. Grace, forgiveness, and personal responsibility are needed for the blessing of a long-lasting, loving relationship.

Discussion/Reflection Questions

1. Alyssa has invested a great deal of time and energy into their daughter McKayla's dance career. Do you think this has any bearing on the marital problems between Alyssa and Brian?

2. Joel has vowed not to be ruined by an alcoholic wife, as his father was by his mother. This would be a deal-breaker for him. Is there anything you consider a deal-breaker in marriage? Does your philosophy agree with the Bible?

3. In the response to the possibly addicted spouse, the counselor says that those who grew up in an atmosphere of addiction have learned to love and excuse an addict's behavior. Is it possible to "unlearn" what we learned as children? If so, how?

4. Were you surprised to learn that research shows snoring as a major contributor to divorce? Why or why not?

5. Deanne seems to be living in a Jekyll and Hyde situation. Should she say something to the church leaders? Why or why not?

6. If you were Deanne's friend, how would you pray for her?

7. Do you agree that Deanne is a major part of the problem?

8. What aspects of your personality or habits have others had to "get over" in order to remain in a peaceful

relationship with you? How does God show you mercy?

9. Have you ever been on the receiving end of passive-aggressive behavior? On the giving end?

10. Olivia wonders how she missed the signs about London. The response shows that the signs were there, but in her optimism, Olivia misread them. Have you ever misread someone (for better or for worse)? How does the Holy Spirit help us to be wise in our dealings with people?

11. Which couple in this section pricked your heart most? Why?

Scriptures for Meditation

Sensible people control their temper; they earn respect by
overlooking wrongs.
Proverbs 19:11

Understand this, my dear brothers and sisters: You must all
be quick to listen, slow to speak, and slow to get angry.
Human anger does not produce the righteousness God
desires.
James 1:19-20

Do to others as you would like them to do to you.
Luke 6:31

Put on then, as God's chosen ones, holy and beloved,
compassionate hearts, kindness, humility, meekness, and
patience, bearing with one another and, if one has a
complaint against another, forgiving each other; as the
Lord has forgiven you, so you also must forgive.
Colossians 3:12-13

Never pay back evil with more evil. Do things in such a
way that everyone can see you are honorable. Do all that
you can to live in peace with everyone. Dear friends, never
take revenge. Leave that to the righteous anger of God.
Romans 12:17-19

Finally, all of you, be like-minded, be sympathetic, love one another, be compassionate and humble. Do not repay evil with evil or insult with insult. On the contrary, repay evil with blessing, because to this you were called so that you may inherit a blessing.
I Peter 3:8-9

And a second is like it: You shall love your neighbor as yourself.
Matthew 22:39

Section Notes

Part 2

Sex

10 - No Sex

Couple: Cameron and Chandra Barnett
Married: 6 years
Children: Twin boys – age 15 (from Chandra's previous marriage)

Chandra avoided malls. She avoided television. She avoided romance novels. She'd even begun avoiding conversations with her sister, Alexis, because Chandra was too embarrassed to admit that she and her second husband, Cameron, had been married six years and she'd been without sex for the past three years.

It started with an injury at work when he'd fallen from the forklift, cracking two bones in his back. It was a miracle he wasn't paralyzed and Chandra had been thankful just to have her husband alive. And she'd understood why they couldn't have sex; Cameron was miserable. But after a surgery and months of physical therapy, he'd been given the "green light" to resume sexual activity.

Chandra remembered splurging at Victoria's Secret and arranging for Alexis to watch the boys for the weekend.

"Going for another set of twins?" Alexis had teased.

Chandra could only laugh then because she really didn't care what happened after she reunited with her husband. If they had quadruplets after that weekend, it would be perfectly fine with her; she just wanted to be intimate with her husband again. Before, their sex life wouldn't have filled the pages of a super-erotic novel, but it had been a major source of enjoyment and security for Chandra. She looked forward to resuming this part of their marriage.

Unfortunately, things hadn't gone as planned that weekend. Cameron was still in a tremendous amount of pain despite the doctors' and therapists' release. They'd tried to take things slow and gentle, but Cameron gave up, apologizing but saying that it was too soon.

That was three years ago. And according to Cameron, it was still "too soon."

No amount of counseling or x-rays seemed to move Cameron past the idea that he was incapable of having sex.

"Don't you *want* to have sex?" she'd asked more than once.

"Of course I do. I just *can't*."

Sometimes, Chandra didn't believe him. She'd researched online the effects of her husband's medications and the emotional toll of traumatic injuries—she realized Cameron had probably thoroughly convinced himself he couldn't have sex anymore. And once he'd made that decision in his mind, he was stubborn enough to believe it.

Yet other times, Chandra knew for certain that Cameron's back was still bothering him. Before the accident, he used to tinker under the hood of his beloved '56 Chevrolet for hours on Saturday mornings. But when he sold it the previous year, he said he physically could not work on it anymore. Chandra realized Cameron's back must have been killing him.

What hurt Chandra most was that the boys, now fifteen, could see their parents weren't affectionate. To them, their parents probably appeared more like roommates. They spoke about logistical matters: who would pick up which child, how much was needed for the water bill, when they planned to meet with the roofing contractor. This wasn't the model Chandra had in mind for the kids, let alone for herself.

No one gets married to be celibate.

Chandra tried to comfort herself with the idea that at least Cameron could still work and contribute to the family financially. The accident could have been much worse; she was grateful at least her husband could walk and talk and change light bulbs around the house. After similar accidents, some others were paralyzed or unconscious in nursing homes.

But what was she going to do—cheat on her husband? Divorce him because he wouldn't or couldn't have sex? She had vowed to love him "in sickness and in health," after all. But how many more years could she take the loneliness and her body's longing to be intimate with him again?

No Sex
Counselor's Commentary

The first question to Chandra would be, "Why haven't you said anything? Why are you attempting to solve a problem that will take both of you to fix?"

Sometimes we suffer in silence, absolutely without reason. Yes we have issues in our relationships, but most of us try to fix them without our spouses. There's no guarantee he would fully understand, validate, or participate in addressing the issue. But not communicating your needs *guarantees* him not participating and not even being aware there is an issue.

Hear Chandra now, "I shouldn't have to say anything! He should already know. He knows we haven't been intimate in years. He's there, too."

If we could read minds there would be far less conflict or far more. Bottom line is that we can't. We must communicate. There's an old saying: A closed mouth doesn't get fed.

Communication is extremely important in a relationship. Talking and listening are the main components to effective communication. Usually both men and women talk. We wait—then we talk again. Rarely do we actually listen to what the other is saying or needing. Although Chandra is trying to approach with caution, she seems to be protecting Cameron's feelings. But is she really?

What if, instead of protecting his feelings, she is not addressing what he needs? What if he needs to discuss his feelings regarding not being able to have sex with her? What if her lack of communication is pushing her further and further away from what she wants most, a connection with her husband?

It doesn't seem fair, does it? He's the head of the household and she is facilitating the solution. Isn't that *his* job? In some circumstances, the answer would be 'yes'. However, she is the one needing resolution and bears the responsibility for effectively communicating this need.

But what is her need? Is it sex? Is it connection with her husband? Is it being a good role model to her children? Is it to have a healthy marriage? Figuring out what she really wants will help in effectively communicating her needs. Effective communication begins with honesty. It's important she is honest in what she truly wants and how she expresses her needs. Telling the partial truth is still a lie. Without honesty, Chandra could ruin any chance of their relationship beginning the journey toward healing. He can't address what he does not know.

This does not mean that she should vent everything she feels or thinks in the name of honesty or getting it all out. Although it may feel great, it could do far more damage and alienate her husband even more. It can be helpful that she speaks so her husband hears her. We often speak so harshly that our intentions and motivations are lost in our delivery.

So what's the solution?

Now that Chandra knows what she wants and effectively communicates, it is up to her to be open to solutions other than her own. He may present issues that she has not considered; he has an experience in the relationship as well. His experience includes him being able to satisfy his wife sexually before the accident; now he may feel embarrassed, insecure, and hopeless. Through this communication the doors may open to a connection with him. They could explore different ways to meet each other's sexual needs. Both should be open to have the conversation that it may look different than it did before, but possible nonetheless. There is fun in creativity. When both feel heard, it strengthens their marriage as well as positively contributes to their efforts in intimacy. This will dismiss any thoughts of turning outside of their marriage to illegitimately meet their sexual needs.

Does this mean she will achieve her goal? Does this guarantee that she will finally have sex?

No, but it does mean she will have a better opportunity to have an intimate connection with her husband. Consequently, they may create an environment that encourages them to find ways to meet their need for sexual fulfillment.

It's worth a try.

11 - Unfulfilling Sex

Couple: Raymond and Elizabeth
Married: 2 years

After a late-night rendezvous, Elizabeth lay awake in bed next to her sleeping husband.

"This can't be normal. Maybe there's something wrong with my body," she thought to herself. After two years—two whole years—she still felt next-to-nothing when she and Raymond made love. More than once, she had considered talking to her gynecologist. All the books she'd read said that it might take time for them to figure out what worked for the two of them in bed. Since Elizabeth had been a virgin when they'd married, she'd accepted it might take a little longer for her than women who had experimented before marriage.

In truth, she'd felt a tingle here and there and did enjoy the emotional closeness of their lovemaking. But when a co-worker said something about how sex was the most amazing thing in the entire universe, Elizabeth cringed inside. She felt cheated as a woman and a Christian who'd waited until marriage, only to be largely disappointed in the experience.

To make matters worse, she was five months pregnant. Total strangers had begun to make comments about her "obvious" joy of sex. In Walmart, a woman said, "Those few minutes of pleasure have a long-term effect, eh?"

Elizabeth had smiled and nodded, wishing she knew exactly what that pleasure was like. *I thought it was only a moment? Is it really two minutes? Why isn't it happening to me?*

The crazy thing was that she didn't want Raymond to know she wasn't sexually satisfied. He seemed so...*into* it. What would happen if she told him that her body didn't think he was all that? And what would he think of her once he learned that she'd been "faking it" by mimicking the sounds and actions she'd witnessed in a few movies and read about in novels?

I have to tell him the truth. We have to work on this.

Elizabeth nudged Raymond once. Twice.

He stirred. "What?"

"I need to talk to you about something."

Instantly, his hand reached for her stomach. "Is everything okay?"

Elizabeth's heart warmed at her husband's caring touch. "Yes. The baby's fine."

Raymond cleared his throat. "What's wrong?"

She could feel him staring at her in the darkness. "It's about sex."

"You wanna do it again?"

"No."

"Oh. Then why'd you wake me up?"

Elizabeth couldn't believe what she was about to say. Was she ready to crush her husband, make him feel like less of a man, ruin their picture-perfect marriage, and expose herself as a liar?

"I was just thinking…how much longer should we keep having sex, with the baby and all." She deceived him for the second time that night.

"I say we just go until we can't go anymore." Raymond laughed. "Nite."

The next morning found Elizabeth up googling various female sexual pleasure statistics. She was in the minority, according to reports. Most regularly sexually active women her age—twenty-four—had experienced orgasm.

Another article said one in every fifteen couples were sexually incompatible. Their bodies just didn't "fit" together. But the point of the article was to persuade couples to consider open marriages. Not an option for Elizabeth and Raymond.

Elizabeth closed her laptop in exasperation. Maybe she was sexually repressed. If so, that would be her parents' fault for raising her to believe her body was a temple, not to be defiled. Was her brain supposed to magically forget all the keep-your-legs-closed lectures the day she got married?

But I don't feel guilty about having sex. It really is beautiful.

And the baby she carried inside was the result of their union, which was nothing less than divine. Raymond was a God-fearing, hard-working man from a good family. He was quite easy on the eyes, too, which made this whole sex thing even more perplexing, because Elizabeth was definitely attracted to him.

She steepled her hands on top of the table. "Lord, I don't know what's wrong, but I need you to help us fix this."

Almost immediately, she knew in her spirit that the first step was to fill Raymond in on the problem.

She fixed his favorite meal and met him at the door when he returned home from work. Raymond always needed about thirty minutes to unwind after a day at the office, so she left him to the television for a while.

When he joined her at the table for dinner, he blessed the food.

Elizabeth decided it best to blurt it out before she lost her nerve. "Ray, what I wanted to tell you last night was that I don't enjoy sex."

His eyebrows drew together. "Huh?"

"I mean, I *like* being intimate with you, but…I've been faking it. I'm sorry. But I know we can—"

"Wait! You've faked it? Every time?"

She nodded.

"Every *single* time?"

Again, Elizabeth nodded.

Raymond dropped his fork on the plate and sat back in his chair. "Well alllllrighty then."

His face bore an expression she had never seen—a mixture of bewilderment, anger, and embarrassment.

The weight of her deceit came crashing down on Elizabeth. "I'm so sorry. I didn't mean to hurt you. I was going to say that I know we can work together and fix this."

Raymond laughed cynically. "I'm not the one with the problem. I've never had any complaints until now."

Elizabeth recognized he was speaking from anger, but his words hurt none the less. They stirred up her insecurities again. *Maybe I really am the problem.*

"I was thinking about talking to my doctor. Probably after the baby is born and my body settles back into its normal state," she said, offering hope.

"Yeah. You let me know how that goes." Raymond grabbed his plate and cup, headed for the den.

He didn't come to bed that night.

In fact, Raymond hadn't come to bed for three nights now. Though he was speaking more and finally answering texts, he hadn't made any advances toward her. And Elizabeth was left to wonder if their sex life would ever improve.

Unfulfilling Sex
Counselor's Commentary

Although Elizabeth and Raymond have issues of sexual intimacy, many other areas of concern that have infiltrated this relationship are communication, expectations, and of course the obvious matter of unfulfilling sex.

Many marriages are silently suffering from the anguish of unmet expectations, mismatched sex drives, or no sex at all. There are varied reasons for these problems. But one that has been the most impactful regarding our intimacy are those of expectations.

So how did we get to the place of unmet expectations in bed?

We are constantly inundated with sexual images and innuendos through social media, television, and music. If we're not careful we'll compare our experiences to these imaginings or even attempt to emulate them.

Hollywood did not create sex nor do filmmakers define it. Unfortunately, we take many cues from this world of scripts, lighting, makeup artists, and body doubles. We have created expectations and requirements that have been written by producers and screenwriters instead of the Word of God. To our chagrin, often we realize that these ideas are selfish in nature and aimed at personal fulfillment only, rather than building a sexual foundation with our spouse.

Consequently, we need to examine and address our own expectations and experiences before trying to analyze or address issues we have prematurely assigned to our spouses. Are our suppositions regarding sex and intimacy aimed at pleasing ourselves and placing blame on our spouses when we're not satisfied? It's our responsibility to develop ourselves personally and spiritually to keep up with the demands of marriage. Through effort, we can transition from the ideas that our spouse is responsible for turning us on to we are responsible for building our intimacy with them.

In the case of Raymond and Elizabeth, it would be helpful to begin by examining their issue of communication regarding sexual experiences in the marriage. Elizabeth will have to accept the responsibility in communicating her concerns to Raymond. He cannot address what he does not know. Her approach to this sensitive subject can welcome his participation or alienate him. As Elizabeth addresses the issue of lack of satisfaction, it will be pivotal to present her complications as a joint effort to examine and resolve. What she should not do is fall into the trap of self-gratification, further alienating her husband from her sexual experience.

We research information to buy houses, cars, and schools for our children. However, we rarely take the time to research to enhance our sexual relationship. For some people this may be a challenging area. Sex may initially seem awkward but dealing with uncomfortable feelings is crucial in developing a strong, mature relationship. She may communicate her desire to initially seek a medical opinion and then experiment sexually to learn her body. She can say "That feels nice, but let's try this." Most men will not have any objections.

Sex was given to use for fulfillment and connection at the deepest level. It is this connection that builds intimacy and partnership.

12 - Perverted Sex

Couple: Stan and LaDonna
Married: 14 years

LaDonna felt the phone vibrate in her pocket while she waited in the express line at Target. She pulled it from her hip and looked at the screen. *Unknown.*

She wished it was true—that she didn't know who was calling. But unfortunately, she did. It was *those people* calling again. The ones she and Stan had begun associating with eighteen months ago, before a co-worker invited her to a women's conference at church and LaDonna began learning about the love of God. LaDonna was no holy roller, but the very idea of a God who loved her and wanted a relationship with her seemed to pull her back to church week after week to learn more of Him. And the more she learned about Him, the more she felt certain that hers and Stan's sex life wasn't pleasing to God.

Of course, Stan wanted nothing to do with this God. "Religion is a man-made crutch to help people who are too weak to cope with reality," her husband had fussed.

Still, he didn't try to stop her from going to church so long as she didn't put much in the offering plate.

Somewhere around that sixth month, however, LaDonna knew she had to make a change. She couldn't keep doing the things she had done with Stan—and others—before. She felt dirty. Used. Even repulsed at the thought of continuing in their swingers group.

Her phone buzzed again.

LaDonna sighed as she checked the number. *Stan.*

"Hey."

"Where are you?"

"At Target. Getting some milk and bread."

"Cool."

She let her hair fall over the left side of her face as she tilted her head to the right. In a hushed tone, she said, "Stan, could you please tell Richard and Amy to stop calling me? Can't they take a hint? I'm *out.*"

"You can't be out. If you're out, I'm out. It's a couples thing. Those are the rules."

Again, LaDonna checked her surroundings before she spoke. "Why can't you just be happy with *me?*"

"I *am* happy with you. But we've been married fourteen years. We need some spice. I don't want to have to cheat on you."

"No one *has* to cheat on *anyone.*" This conversation was turning her stomach as sour as the gallon of milk she'd poured out that morning.

"LaDonna, come on! We're both into it."

She clenched her teeth. "Stan, I'm perfectly content with you and you alone. This whole thing is just…wrong. I mean, there's a reason why we can't tell our friends, our family, or anyone who actually respects us about what we're doing. We certainly can't post it on Facebook. Isn't that a clue?"

Stan sighed. "I swear, I had no idea I was married to such a prude."

She wanted to be angry with her husband, but how could she? Stan had married a woman who'd always been sexually adventurous.

LaDonna moved forward in line and placed her two items on the counter. "Hold on, Stan."

The cashier briefly acknowledged her and scanned the items. LaDonna handed over a ten dollar bill, then took the change and the plastic bags on her way out of the store.

"I'm back. Look, Babe. I love you. But I'm out. I want you to tell them to stop. Calling. Me. And they should stop calling you, too. Rules are rules."

"I'm staying in, LaDonna. Even if I have to bring someone else. It's just sex."

She opened the door to her SUV and placed the two sacks on the passenger's seat.

"So that's our decision?" she asked point-blank. "You're going to continue to have sex with other people without me?"

"You leave me no choice."

"Really?"

"Really."

She sighed. "I gotta go."

When Stan made it home from work, he didn't press the issue.

They ate dinner and watched television as usual until it was time for showers and bed. That's when Stan fired up the DVD and offered to play one of their all-time favorite porn videos.

"Stan. I really don't want those images in my head anymore," LaDonna protested, though she knew Stan couldn't fathom why watching was a problem if the people on screen weren't physically in their bedroom.

"I can't take this anymore. You've absolutely lost your mind. I'm not going to be married to some Bible-thumping chick who won't even try to meet my needs. Isn't that in the Bible, too—meet your husband's needs? By any means necessary," Stan fumed.

"Um, that last part is, like, Malcolm X, I think."

Stan sat on the edge of the bed. "I have no idea how we're going to make it."

LaDonna shrugged. "Maybe we won't."

Perverted Sex
Counselor's Commentary

So at first glance we may want to think that LaDonna and Stan are dealing with issues related to their sex life and a changing perspective due to her accepting Christ. We also might assume the issue is how do they deal with his actions and if her responsibility to him is to participate or support him.

Although these issues are important we have to address the overarching situation. Interestingly enough, this is not rare. Many people marry as unbelievers, and eventually one accepts life in Christ and the other is left wondering what happened. In this situation, the wife is the one who becomes the believer first. However, there is a case to make that there are some men who decide to open their hearts to the Lord and pray for their wives to make the same decision. In any order, one spouse accepting Christ is more common than we know.

LaDonna is now in a position where she is married to an unbeliever. Unfortunately for Stan this is not who he married and not what he asked for. Now he is contending with her changing right before his eyes. The many differences he must face will surely cause conflict and eventually a decision.

There is comfort in knowing that this did not just happen. This situation did not catch God by surprise. This is by divine design. It is important LaDonna realizes this truth.

At this point it is up to LaDonna to be realistic regarding her expectations of her husband. It is counterproductive for her to expect him to immediately adapt her view and accept these drastic changes within her. She should understand that because she has accepted Christ, it may not be automatic that he will accept her changes or Christ. Knowing that her decision affects not only her choices sexually, but her approach to their marriage, she should expect some resistance. This may be evident through his words or actions as he continues to question and challenge her.

Having unrealistic expectations of her husband's response will cause her to experience anger, frustration, resentment, and eventually depression. She must realize that her decisions are solely hers and this may not in any way influence his decision to stop swinging.

At this point in the relationship, LaDonna has made a choice based upon her faith not to participate. Now she must communicate this decision but express her love for her husband and marriage. She has to make sure she expresses her commitment to honoring him in being committed to their marriage.

It is easy to think that the recommendation is for her to sit, pray, and wait. Scripture tells us "let the unbeliever leave." It also tells us that divorce is permitted if he leaves or continues to have affairs.

So now what? What if he doesn't leave? What if he doesn't decide to stop having sex with others?

What should she do?

She should do nothing to pressure him to make a biblical choice. He is not governed by God's Word. Romans 8:7 lets us know that the carnal mind is hostile toward God. It is not subject to the law of God, neither can it be.

At the time she expresses her decision and her unwillingness to participate, it becomes her husband's decision to either accept it or not. Based on how he responds to her new Godly standard, LaDonna will know her next step.

It is recommended that she seeks the support of a Christian counselor to navigate her next step. It is vital she has someone walking with her and guiding her with the truth of God's Word through this formidable process. As LaDonna works through this, she should be an example of scripture that explains how her husband is won without a word. How she responds to him outside of the sex during this time is crucial. Preaching to him and constantly nagging at him will eventually drive him away from the very decision that she desperately wants him to make.

Discussion/Reflection Questions

1. Chandra and Cameron haven't been physically intimate for three years. Now she feels neglected, resentful, and wonders how she will remain faithful. What would you pray if another believer shared this secret with you?

2. Why do you think Elizabeth felt the need to fake her satisfaction in bed?

3. How can parents/elders warn youth of the perils of premarital sex without negatively impacting the post-marital sex life?

4. LaDonna is trying to change the foundation of her marriage with Stan, but he's not having it. Does this seem like an impossible situation? How can God still be glorified in LaDonna's life no matter what Stan decides?

5. Which points in the counselor's commentaries impacted you most?

Scriptures for Meditation

Certainly—but only within a certain context. It's good for a man to have a wife, and for a woman to have a husband. Sexual drives are strong, but marriage is strong enough to contain them and provide for a balanced and fulfilling sexual life in a world of sexual disorder. The marriage bed must be a place of mutuality—the husband seeking to satisfy his wife, the wife seeking to satisfy her husband. Marriage is not a place to "stand up for your rights." Marriage is a decision to serve the other, whether in bed or out. Abstaining from sex is permissible for a period of time if you both agree to it, and if it's for the purposes of prayer and fasting—but only for such times. Then come back together again. Satan has an ingenious way of tempting us when we least expect it. I'm not, understand, commanding these periods of abstinence—only providing my best counsel if you should choose them.
1 Corinthians 7:2-6 (The Message Bible)

Let marriage be held in honor among all, and let the marriage bed be undefiled, for God will judge the sexually immoral and adulterous.
Hebrews 13:4

Flee from sexual immorality. Every other sin a person commits is outside the body, but the sexually immoral person sins against his own body.
1 Corinthians 6:18

Therefore a man shall leave his father and his mother and hold fast to his wife, and they shall become one flesh.
Genesis 2:24

Let your fountain be blessed, and rejoice in the wife of your youth, a lovely deer, a graceful doe. Let her breasts fill you at all times with delight; be intoxicated always in her love.
Proverbs 5:18-19

But because of the temptation to sexual immorality, each man should have his own wife and each woman her own husband.
1 Corinthians 7:2

For this is the will of God, your sanctification: that you abstain from sexual immorality; that each one of you know how to control his own body in holiness and honor, not in the passion of lust like the Gentiles who do not know God;
1 Thessalonians 4:3-5

Section Notes

_____

_____

_____

_____

_____

_____

_____

_____

_____

_____

_____

_____

_____

_____

_____

_____

_____

_____

_____

_____

Part 3

Expectations

13 - Scripting Spouse

Couple: Drake and Michelle
Married: 2 years

Michelle sat across the table from her husband, Drake, at a booth in a restaurant that happened to boast gigantic television screens dropping down from every direction. All channels were set on ESPN, the NFL channel, or the NBA channel, which obviously made it hard for Drake to concentrate on what Michelle was saying.

"Are you listening?" She clanked her glass with a fork.

Drake tore his gaze from screen number three. "Yes. I hear you."

"Thank you. As I was saying—"

"They're making arrangements to donate Paris's organs. I heard you," Drake repeated her exact words.

"Yes." Michelle took a deep breath, assured that he was actually listening. "But before you can take the organs, you have to officially declare a person dead. And as soon as that happens, the news reporters will eat it up. And there will be this whole media frenzy before half the family is even notified that she's dead."

Drake's eyes flitted toward the screen for a second, then back to Michelle.

He nodded in agreement with her.

"What do you think of that?" she asked.

"What do I think of what?"

Michelle slammed her hand on the table, causing both plates to bounce slightly. "I knew you weren't listening!"

"Calm down. I heard you—that's a tough dilemma."

Satisfied again, she asked, "What *else* do you think?"

He frowned in thought. "Umm…nothing. I mean, if it happens that would be bad. But they do need to harvest the organs quickly, so I get the time constraints."

"But what do you *think* of it?"

"I'm not thinking anything, Michelle. Nothing. It is what it is. What do *you* think of it?" He turned the tables.

She had an answer ready on her lips. "I think it's awful. The way the laws and the medical field are—it's like they didn't think things through."

Drake said, "Okay." He took another bite of tilapia.

"I don't even know why I try talking to you," Michelle fussed. She wiped her lips with the linen napkin and set it on the table. "I've lost my appetite."

"Seriously?"

She smacked, "Yeah. I'm done here."

Drake grabbed her hand underneath the table. "Babe. Don't do this. It's our anniversary. The night's just getting started." He pumped his eyebrows—their secret signal for sex.

Michelle's heart plunged as she realized her husband was no longer thinking of her sweet third cousin, Paris, who'd been hit by a drunk driver who happened to be the mayor's son.

Drake wasn't even thinking about the fact that they'd made it through their first two years of marriage. He was thinking about sex. Of all things, *sex*.

"Drake, I really, really want us to have a great marriage. I want us to have a connection. To be best friends. But it's so hard sometimes," she gushed, holding back tears so she wouldn't make any more of a scene.

"I *am* your friend. Our marriage is great," he said, squeezing her hand. "What do you want from me?"

"I want you to *be here* for me."

His brows knit together. "I *am* here."

"Yeah, but I don't feel like you're *in this* with me. Sharing the emotions, the feelings. To-ge-ther."

He sighed helplessly. "I'm don't know how to be any more *here* than I am right now."

Michelle shook her head because, just then, she realized that unfortunately, Drake was telling the truth.

The Scripting Spouse
Counselor's Commentary

We can hear Michelle. Can't you? She just wants to connect!

She understands that Drake can hear her, too, but is he really *listening* with his whole heart? Why can't he reach down deep inside her soul and fill the hole she's been walking around with for a while? Then, they'd really be able to connect. Right?

Michelle used the word "connection," but what she really wants is emotional intimacy. Emotional intimacy exists when there is a deep sense of trust and healthy communication in a relationship. It produces a place of safety, one where our deepest, private self and all of its faults are accepted and loved relentlessly. This is a place where a woman feels she is loved like Christ loves the church and gave Himself for it as in Ephesians 5.

Isn't that what Michelle wants? Isn't that what we all want?

Women are nurturers who desire to be nurtured. We're our best selves when we feel our relationships with the people we love are satisfying and fruitful. We are validated by our relationships. Our identity and worth are often intertwined in their success. Our identity and self worth are validated through good feelings associated with the success of these relationships. As a result, some of us take it upon ourselves to manufacture this emotional intimacy. We require the people around us to read their lines and play their parts in our self-prescribed scripts. When our loved ones go off-script, we may find ourselves feeling unsafe and helpless.

Some would look at Drake and Michelle's marriage and think their lack of connectivity has to be his fault. She needs him to engage and he is not equipped to catch her clues. Yes, he needs lessons in listening 101, but let's challenge our tendency towards safety and look at this a little differently.

If we went deeper we would see Michelle picked the wrong time and place to have an intimate and heavy conversation. Yes, it is their anniversary and they have had a recent family tragedy. However, they are sitting in a restaurant with the distraction of televisions and sports. Timing is important. Michelle is competing for his attention and is, unfortunately, losing.

Assessing reality is extremely important in establishing intimacy. We must take a sober look at behavior vs. expectation. It would not be too far away from reality to assume Drake is not driven by emotional intimacy. Michelle may have been so intent on her script she could have ignored behaviors that indicated his difficulty with emotionally connecting. She could have placed faith in her own ability to nurture and hoped her shining example would equip and motivate him towards emotional intimacy.

So. Michelle has finally stepped outside of her script and admitted her reality. She has a disconnected marriage and possibly a husband who is either unable or unwilling to place effort into deep emotional connection.

If only there was a great list of seven ways to establish emotional intimacy, a quick fix hope. But there is no such package. Yet it would be unfortunate to not offer any encouragement at all. This would leave the assumption our deepest need will never be met.

The only reasonable solution for Michelle that will work without fail is for her to begin the journey of intimacy through establishing a deeper connection with God. Sometimes we are so dead set on requiring others to meet our expectations, we eliminate the most tried and true option—turning towards our Heavenly Father to meet our needs. Filtering (or abandoning) our scripts through God's Word is an opportunity for us to grow spiritually and emotionally. It facilitates peace within ourselves and in our marriages. Once Michelle consistently experiences the safety of God's love, she will demand it less from mere humans.

Second, she must learn how to establish an authentic relationship with the man Drake *is* and stop demanding a deep connection with the idea of the man she thinks he *should* be. To continue pursuing her script would be to self-inflict unwanted pain and rejection.

To begin the journey of deeper connection and a rewarding relationship, we must make an effort to learn each other as-is and allow room for God's Word and for the other's shortcomings. Having a safe place in the relationship to explore our vulnerabilities and expose our faults will establish a place of trust and a willingness to grow.

In most cases this takes time and help from a relationship professional. When we are in a place of disconnect, it's an effort in futility to take on this challenge alone. Having well-equipped support to traverse such a fragile season in our marriage would be beneficial. A third party might help us empathize, understand, and gain insight to obtain what we want most.

One last note: If you are the "Drake," whose spouse has an irrational expectation of you filling the space that only God can fill in their heart, you may also choose to seek the help of a professional Christian counselor. They may guide you in setting boundaries and not taking on a role you were never intended to handle. You will be better equipped to assist your spouse to look to Jesus to meet their needs. If your spouse is not at that place where they want to seek the help of a professional together, it is best to seek help on your own.

14 - Unbelieving Spouse

Couple: Mark and Toni Smith
Married: 9 years
Children: Brittany – age 7; Dustin – age 5

The chances of Dustin getting into RightWay Academy had been slim to none. Toni couldn't believe the letter she was reading now.

Mr. and Mrs. Smith,

We are pleased to inform you that Dustin Smith has been accepted into RightWay Academy's kindergarten program.

"Yes," she screamed, which brought the kids running into the kitchen.

"What?" Brittney panted.

"Dustin. Honey, you got into RightWay!"

His eyes widened. "I did?"

"Yes. You'll start this fall."

Brittney gave her younger brother a high-five.

Toni was sure Dustin had little idea of how important this was—she hadn't wanted him to feel academic pressure before he even started school. She'd only told him he was going "to talk to some people about school stuff" the day of the evaluation. Dustin had been nervous, but he eventually warmed up enough for the team of diagnosticians to assess where he stood on the autistic spectrum.

Though RightWay was a school for students with a variety of special needs, they only had so many slots for kids with autism. Toni hadn't learned about the school until January, which had put them way down on the waiting list. But God!

"Hey guys—let's pray," Toni suggested as she held out both hands. The children latched on and she led the prayer. "God, we thank You for opening the door for a school that's just right for Dustin. We pray that he will have a successful kindergarten year and that You will grace him for everything he needs to learn. In Jesus' name we pray, amen."

"Amen, the children repeated."

Later, Mark hadn't been quite as enthused when Toni called him to share the news. "That's the private school, right?"

"Yep. They've got a much better program than what I've seen in public schools. I mean, Brittney's school is fine for her, but they just don't have the resources to help Dustin."

"We gotta do what we gotta do."

Toni was happy to hear him agree.

"How much is that gonna run us?"

"They've got a sliding scale. It's gonna cost us about four hundred a month. But don't worry. I've already thought of some ways to cut back. Plus, I believe that since

God allowed Dustin to get into RightWay, I'm sure He will make a way for us to keep him there."

"I don't know what God's got to do with this, but I agree it's the best school for him. We'll make it happen."

"Love you." Toni disconnected the call and tried to forget what Mark had said about God.

She carried on with the evening routine, getting the kids fed, bathed, and settled before Mark got home from work. When he arrived, the kids tackled him at the door. Toni watched, amused by the relationship her children were developing with their father.

Toni warmed Mark's plate in the microwave.

After a few minutes of wrestling, Mark sat at the table.

"Dad, will you play Wii with us tonight?" Brittney asked.

"Sure. Let me eat first."

He kissed Toni as she set his plate before him.

Toni returned to the kitchen to finish the dishes.

The kids scrambled back to the family room, but Dustin must have been keeping an eye on Mark because Toni overheard him say to Brittney, "Dad didn't say his grace."

To which Brittney frankly replied, "He doesn't say grace."

"Why not?"

"He just doesn't."

Toni interrupted them, yelling across the bar area, "Guys, why don't you go ahead and start the games, get in a little extra practice so you can beat dad."

As soon as Mark finished eating, the whole family played a few rounds of bowling before it was time for Brittney and Dustin to go to their rooms.

This was exactly what Toni had envisioned her life would be like—a stay-at-home mom, devoted to her husband and children, managing her household. She had a loving, hard-working husband and great kids. It was all picture-perfect.

Except for one thing: Toni was a believer. Mark wasn't.

That night when she and Mark climbed into their king-sized sleigh bed, the spiritual chasm between them echoed loudly.

Mark flipped on the television and started watching an action movie, rife with profanity.

"Could you turn that down?"

Mark grabbed the remote from the nightstand.

Toni watched as the volume menu appeared on the screen and the number of bars descended from seven to four.

"You okay now, baby Jesus?"

Toni pulled her Christian book from the nightstand and began reading, though the constant barrage of curse words and the graphic killing scenes interrupted the edifying words on the final pages of her Kim Cash Tate novel.

Unlike the book's characters, Toni hadn't been concerned much that Mark wasn't a Christian when they married. He was nice, kind, and smart—not to mention his Colgate smile. When she'd asked him about his faith, thanks to a book with 100 questions to ask before marrying, his response had been, "I mean, yeah, I think there's a God. Somewhere. Out there, I guess."

And that was enough for her. He wasn't exactly an atheist. Though Toni had spent many Sundays in church, she didn't read her Bible regularly or pray or do a lot of things she was supposed to do back then, either, so who was she to judge?

But now that she had come to know God intimately and see His works in even the smallest things doctors said Dustin would not be able to do, Toni was quickly falling in love with Jesus. She wondered how much longer it would be before this faith-gap between her and Mark became impossible to span. How much longer before she grew so close to Christ that she was miles away from her husband?

What scared her even more was the question of how much longer until Dustin or Brittney decided that they wanted to stay home from church, like the father they adored?

What will I do then, God?

Unbelieving Spouse
Counselor's Commentary

Being unequally yoked is an issue that many of us are facing within our marriages. Some married as unbelievers, but one spouse accepted Christ as their Savior along the way while the other maintains their unbelief. In many homes, they are both in Christ but one may grow spiritually at a different pace. Or, as in the case of Toni, some were immature Christians who did not heed the warning in 2 Corinthians 6:14 to avoid partnering with those who do not believe.

In any case, these situations cause much strife and discord. Some question whether or not they made the right decision in marrying. They wonder if they can follow a husband who is an unbeliever. Some even question whether or not they should remain married.

Even though there is great importance in the spiritual life of a family, an unbelieving spouse is in no way a reason to cancel the covenant made in marriage.

"If any brother has a wife who is not a believer and she is willing to live with him, he must not divorce her. And if a woman has a husband who is not a believer and he is willing to live with her, she must not divorce him." (1 Corinthians 7:12-13)

In Mark and Toni's situation, she has grown in her faith and is experiencing concern regarding her husband's actions and how it may impact her children. She asks herself, "What will I do then"?

The first thing we attempt to do when there is a problem in marriage is try to come up with solutions to fix it. One tendency is to try to coerce the unbelieving spouse into a relationship with God. "Maybe if I invite the pastor over then he can speak with him. What if I have a family Bible study? What if I buy him a book of spiritual leadership in the family? What about a conversation on his role as a father?"

There may be overt attempts to have countless conversations that will hopefully grip the husband's heart and yank him into the fold of believers. Fearful that things might not change soon enough, the believing spouse might also try to use guilt, condemnation, or even plots involving the children to win the sinner's heart.

But the truth is: There is nothing a wife can say that will suddenly convince her husband to accept Christ. The prompting to repent and receive the Lord comes from Him (John 6:44).

Well, let's give Toni a little relief. God wants her husband to believe even more than she does. He doesn't want anyone to perish (2 Peter 3:9). Her only responsibility in this situation is that she continues to be the wife that the Lord has called her to be. Her efforts to change Mark will be futile and frustrating. It is much simpler to allow herself to release him to God and allow the Lord to access his heart through her actions.

She must continue to fulfill her call to her husband as well as her family. If she is not careful, as a result of failed attempts to convert her husband, Toni can easily become resentful or even begin to reject Mark. Therefore, she must continue to have a submissive heart to her husband as stated in I Peter 3:1 "Likewise, wives, be subject to your own husbands, so that even if some do not obey the word, they may be won without a word by the conduct of their wives."

As for her children, through her actions she can demonstrate the love God has for us. She can love Mark through her respect for him in her relationship with him as well as in his relationship with the children. She must not act or verbalize her disapproval of him to her children or allow them to dishonor or disrespect their father.

And finally, Toni must also pray for her husband and not give way to despair or self-pity. She must let go of her sense of responsibility to "save" him. The power of prayer is her greatest spiritual influence on her husband. There is no one in a better spiritual position to pray for her husband than Toni. This is her most valuable source of strength and hope. She must pray for him and intercede where the enemy would use this situation as an opportunity to divide their home.

Discussion/Reflection Questions

1. Which couple reminded you most of your marriage or the marriages that you have had an opportunity to observe closely? Why?

2. Michelle has a "script" that she expects others to follow precisely. She becomes upset when people don't do what she wants them to do. Could you relate to Michelle? Why or why not? How does God respond when you don't do exactly what He wants you to do?

3. The advice for Michelle is to establish a deep relationship with God that will sustain her even when others won't (or in Drake's case doesn't have the capacity to) do so. Is God really enough in your life? Do you turn to Him first for comfort, peace, or a listening ear? Why or why not?

4. As Toni's love for God grows, she feels as though she has less in common with her husband. On a scale of 1-10 (1 being not vital, 10 paramount), how important do you think it is to be married to someone who shares your faith to the same degree?

5. What special challenges do you think those who are unequally yoked face in a marriage?

6. Consider couples that start off equally yoked, but one spouse fails to continue to grow spiritually. How might you encourage one or both spouses?

Scriptures for Meditation

The righteous cry out, and the Lord hears them;
he delivers them from all their troubles.
The Lord is close to the brokenhearted
and saves those who are crushed in spirit.
The righteous person may have many troubles,
but the Lord delivers him from them all;
Psalm 34: 17-19

Surely the righteous will never be shaken;
they will be remembered forever.
They will have no fear of bad news;
their hearts are steadfast, trusting in the Lord.
Their hearts are secure, they will have no fear;
in the end they will look in triumph on their foes.
Psalm 112:6-8

Enjoy life with your wife, whom you love, all the days
of this meaningless life that God has given you under the
sun—all your meaningless days. For this is your lot in life
and in your toilsome labor under the sun.
Ecclesiastes 9:9

So do not fear, for I am with you;
do not be dismayed, for I am your God.
I will strengthen you and help you;

I will uphold you with my righteous right hand.
Isaiah 41:10

Be completely humble and gentle; be patient, bearing with one another in love. Make every effort to keep the unity of the Spirit through the bond of peace.
Ephesians 4:2-3

The end of all things is near. Therefore be alert and of sober mind so that you may pray. Above all, love each other deeply, because love covers over a multitude of sins. Offer hospitality to one another without grumbling.
1 Peter 4:7-10

Section Notes

_____

_____

_____

_____

_____

_____

_____

_____

_____

_____

_____

_____

_____

_____

_____

_____

_____

_____

_____

_____

_____

_____

_____

Part 4
Family Dynamics

15 - In-Laws

Couple: Evan and Jada Willis
Married: 16 years
Children: Lynelle – age 9

Jada rang the doorbell at her sister-in-law's house once. Twice. Three times. Still no answer. Jada looked over both shoulders, checking her surroundings before pulling her iPhone from her purse. She had grown up in a less-than-ideal neighborhood like this one. Though she and Evan were living on the "right" side of the tracks now, she still knew how to watch her back in a high-crime area.

She laughed to herself, thinking, *You can take the girl out of the hood, but you can't take the hood out of the girl.*

Convinced that her surroundings were clear, she dialed her daughter's cell phone.

"Hi, Momma."

"Lynelle, honey, I'm here to pick you up."

"Okay."

Seconds later, Lynelle opened the door with her cousin, Zaria, at her side. The two looked like they could have been sisters, which warmed Jada's heart. Lynelle was an only child, born after years of miscarriages, fertility treatments, and heartbreak. Even now, Jada was overcome with thanksgiving at the sight of her daughter.

"Hey, girls!" She hugged her daughter and niece, stepping inside the house.

"Hi, Auntie Jada. Sorry, the doorbell doesn't work."

Jada withheld her question: *Why won't your mom fix it?* Instead, she asked, "Where's Andre?"

"He's with his dad."

She heard Evan's sister, Daniyah, call, "Who's at the door?"

And then Jada wondered: *Why would you let the kids go to the door if you didn't even know who it was?*

"It's Auntie Jada," Zaria yelled back.

"Oh. Hey!"

Jada followed the voice to the kitchen, where Daniyah was braiding a man's hair in cornrows.

Jada had never seen the man before. He had to be in his mid-30s, arms tatted up and down, and he faintly smelled of marijuana.

"Sup?" the man addressed Jada, his eyes traveling up and down her body.

She stood up straight and covered her midsection with her Michael Khors bag. "Hello."

Daniyah said, "The girls had a good time. Stayed up all night listening to music and dancing. I'm still surprised you let Lynelle come over."

Jada didn't miss the smirk on Daniyah's face. "Well, they *are* first cousins."

"We went to McDonalds yesterday. Everybody thought they were twins." Daniyah laughed. "If Momma was still alive, she'd have them dressed alike every day. I promise you."

Jada smiled. "I know, right?"

Daniyah grabbed the rattail comb from the table and parted the man's hair.

Jada tried to talk herself out of being too critical. She knew that braiding hair was her sister-in-law's source of income and that she did it in her home. Jada just hadn't thought about the fact some of those clients might be men, and that they'd be sitting in the house while Lynelle was over for a visit. This scenario didn't fare well with Jada, but now wasn't the time to address it.

"We're gonna get on home now," Jada announced. "Thanks for keeping her."

"Any time."

I don't think so.

Jada hugged her niece good-bye. She and Lynelle got into the car and headed back to their home. "Did you have fun?"

"Yes. Me and Zaria stayed up until three o'clock!"

"Wow." *That's crazy.* "So...Aunt Daniyah said you guys stayed up listening to music all night?"

"Yeah, we were listening to music. But then we got bored. So we turned on the TV and watched some movies."

"Movies like what?"

"One of 'em was, like, this girl...and her boyfriend got her pregnant..."—Jada held her breath—"but he was really an alien, so the baby was a monster and he stabbed everybody in the house except his mom. It was really scary. That's why we stayed up so late—we were too scared to go to sleep." Lynelle giggled innocently.

Jada was at a loss for words. "Ummm...do you remember the name of the movie?"

"I think it was...Strange Crib."

Strange Crib! Jada had seen the previews on television several months ago. That movie was rated PG-13. Obviously, Daniyah had no kind of parental block on her cable television despite the fact Zaria and her younger brother lived there.

"So then when we couldn't go to sleep, we just started watching music videos. Dancing."

Jada didn't even want to ask what all they'd seen in the videos. Her heart was still pounding from the words that had come from her baby's mouth. *Boyfriend. Pregnant. Stabbed.*

Jada put on a happy face and guided Lynelle up to her bedroom when they got home. Jada needed to put some distance between her child and the conversation she was about to have with Evan when he got home from watching the game at a friend's house.

As soon as he walked through the door, it was on. "Evan. We have to talk."

He'd barely had a moment to hook his keys on the holder to the right of the frame. "Okaaaaay."

"Your sister allowed Lynelle to watch a disturbing movie. And music videos showing only God-knows-what."

"Okaaay. I mean." He shrugged, "It's Daniyah's house. We can't tell her what to do in her own house."

Jada shook her head in disbelief. "Are you kidding me? She also had a *man* in the house."

"A boyfriend?"

"No. Some guy. She was braiding his hair. He was probably high."

"Braiding hair is her occupation. And she was sitting there with the man, right?"

Again, Evan seemed to brush Jada off with a shrug. He walked toward the kitchen and opened the refrigerator, apparently searching for a late snack in the middle of the crisis.

"Evan. Are you listening to me? *This* is crazy! *This* is why I don't deal with your family."

He closed the refrigerator, empty-handed. "What do you want me to do? Call her and tell her to block her TV and shut down her business when Lynelle comes over?"

"Uh, no. You don't have to tell her anything because Lynelle is not going back over there again. Ever. Not until your sister gets some kind of common sense or takes a parenting class."

"Wait. Whoa." Evan held up his hands like a stop sign. "My sister is all the family I got left."

"No. *Lynelle and I* are your family." Jada pointed at herself and then upstairs.

"Jada. You're overreacting. My sister loves Lynelle. No harm was done."

"You're *under*-reacting. But I shouldn't be surprised. This is how you are with your family. *Always* taking up for them." Out of respect for her deceased mother-in-law, Jada stopped just short of bringing up how Evan had always taken his mother's side when they'd had run-ins in the past.

"Well, if you don't want to let Lynelle see her cousin Zaria again, that news is going to have to come from you." Evan took off for their bedroom.

"Don't put me in the middle of this." Jada followed him.

"You put *yourself* in the middle of it. I'm out."

He started his shower water and left her on the bed pouting.

In-Laws
Counselor's Commentary

When we marry, we not only become connected with the one we love most. We also join an entire new system of strangers our spouse calls family.

"How did my sweet husband that I connect with so well come from these people?" These are the sentiments of some. Others are blessed with great relationships with in-laws and the transition into the new family is seamless.

Not so with Jada and Evan.

In-law relationships are always interesting to establish at the beginning of our marital journey. Cultivating new bonds with extended family members can be exciting while tremendously difficult.

When we marry, we must realize and accept that we are coming in on relationships, communication styles, and behaviors that have been established and validated for years. They have recognized, ignored, fixed, or even continued unhealthy dynamics. Realize that our role in this new situation is not to come in and enlighten them to our ways. Although we may feel they may need guidance, it is not our duty to place our ways or family patterns as the goal to be achieved.

Many of us are used to a style of belonging in our own families and it is difficult to adapt to new family styles. Non-verbal, verbal cues, and communication styles are different. Respect and privacy are defined differently. Parenting styles and family loyalty are also viewed from different perspectives and experiences.

Although Jada and Evan are communicating about family issues, they are arguing from two different sets of family rules and expectations. Jada wants Evan to tell his sister to adopt her style of living and parenting if she wants to have a relationship with her daughter. Evan wants Jada to disregard her concerns and establish the same trust in his sister that he has had throughout his life. Both are requiring the other to validate their feelings and adopt their viewpoint. There is no winner in this situation when both are trying to force their context as the one and only. They should have the discussion about family conflict and set rules when handling in-law problems before conflict occurs.

Rules might include:

1. Have the discussion alone and not in the presence of their children or in-laws.

2. Listen with empathy and try to gain an understanding of the other's perspective and feelings.

3. Establish and implement a plan of reasonable compromise.

4. Remember that there are no sides. The goal is to work together—not win the argument.

Although Jada has concerns regarding the parenting style and lifestyle of her sister-in-law, it is important that she does not impose her lifestyle and personal preferences as requirements for relationships. She can accept that her sister-in-law has differences in her life and parenting. Evan and Jada will need to arrive at a compromise that doesn't impose Jada's lifestyle on Daniyah, but also doesn't put Lynelle at risk for exposure to inappropriate situations.

Once she and Evan talk and arrive at a mutual agreement, Evan can then share his concerns with his sister on behalf of his household. They should not be presented as a condemnation or questioning of Daniyah's parenting skills or a disregard for her lifestyle.

Jada must accept that trying to control people or circumstances that are out of her control only makes her appear unstable and out of control. She must put her trust in God's ability to parent and protect her child at all times. As parents, we must understand that we cannot dictate or control every situation in or around our children. In our presence or our absence, we must trust that the Lord can teach and protect far better than we can.

16 - Step-Parenting

Couple: Lonnie and Sheila Riley
Married: 5 years
Children: Jackson – age 16 (Lonnie's son who lives with his mother); Luke – age 10 (Sheila's son from a previous marriage)

Sheila dreaded report-card day even more than her son, Luke. Fifth grade was turning out to be quite a challenge for him, especially math. She remembered her own frustration with fractions and decimals at Luke's age and how she'd struggled through the concepts until, one day, it was like the mathematical light came on and she finally *got* it. She was praying that the magic light would shine on Luke soon, too.

But when he walked out of the school's gym with his head held down, Sheila knew immediately that the math-light hadn't flashed on her son that day.

Slowly, he slid into the back seat. "Made a fifty-five on the test. So I'm gonna be grounded by tomorrow."

Sheila's heart sank as she fought back tears. "Oh, no, honey. I'm so sorry."

Through the rearview mirror, Sheila saw her son cross his arms and try to hold his own tears at bay. "I hate math. I hate school. I'm stupid!"

"No, you're not, Luke. You can do this. I'm gonna see about getting you a tutor."

Luke swiped a tear from his face.

"It'll be okay." She tried to assure him, although she already knew her husband wouldn't agree.

Later that night, after Luke was asleep, she waited in bed for her husband's return from his late evening workout.

"How was the gym?"

"Good. No craziness in the evenings, you know?"

"Yeah."

"Honey, I want to talk to you about something," she ventured, closing the women's devotional she was reading and setting it on the nightstand.

"What?" Lonnie peeled the sweat-soaked shirt off his muscular torso.

"Luke. He got another bad grade on a math test today. When the teacher records it in the system, he's gonna have a failing grade for the six weeks."

Lonnie shook his head, ducked into the bathroom and turned on the shower water.

Sheila waited for his return, knowing that he always let the water run a few minutes before jumping in.

Seconds later, he returned and opened his top drawer, searching for night clothes.

"Did you hear me?"

"Of course. I'm not deaf. What do you want me to say? I've already given you a solution."

"Luke is struggling, Lonnie. Discipline isn't the answer to everything."

Lonnie shook his head. "You're making him soft. But that's not my problem. That's for you and Mike to worry about when he gets older. I told you—if he was *my* son, I'd take it out on his behind. We wouldn't have any more problems, guaranteed."

"What do you mean, *if* he was your son? He *is* your son—we're a package deal, remember?" Sheila stood and joined him at the dresser.

Lonnie finally stared down at her face. "Then if he's part of my package, why don't you let me handle him *my* way?"

"Do you really think that spanking him will somehow make him understand fractions better?"

"You can learn a lot when your behind is on the line. Got that from my dad and the military. And Jackson got it from me, too. That's why he's a straight-A student. He knows if he brings home anything less than his best, he'll have to answer to me. You have to set expectations, Sheila, or Luke will never amount to anything."

She rubbed Lonnie's bare shoulder. "I know that's how you feel, but I'm telling you—math is hard on some people. I looked it up on the internet. It's got to do with where you are developmentally."

Lonnie laughed. "That's what's wrong with the world today. People making up all these excuses for why their kids are failing. Got a syndrome for everything and a pill for it, too. You're making him soft, Sheila."

Sheila wasn't in the mood for another argument, so she walked back to bed. Lonnie took his shower.

When he tried to reach for her, she played sleep to avoid the good-night kiss.

Step-Parenting
Counselor's Commentary

Perhaps the two most important relationships in blended families are husband and wife, and the step-parents to step-children. It's important to understand that without working to establish healthy relationships, there will be stress, conflict, and building resentment.

Blending families is very common, but few people actually prepare to be a step-parent. Even though most who are accepting the "package deal" feel as though they are willing and equipped to take on the challenge, they soon learn that they are ill-prepared for the complexities of this relationship. They assume that a few interactions and spending time together is a guarantee of mutual respect and long-lasting relationships. What they have not considered is the fact that when parents remarry, the family has grown and now the child has to reorganize their hearts and loyalties.

The biggest mistake that biological parents make in these relationships is that they assume their children are just as in love with the person and just as excited to welcome someone else into their lives. Children are not partners in the adult relationship. They don't understand the dynamics of marriage. They often are unsure regarding how the "new" parent fits in with their biological parent relationships.

Additionally, children find difficulty in trying to replicate the same relationships with step-parents as they have or had with their biological parents. Children at any age may demonstrate behavior changes as well as regression. It is irresponsible to assume that the package deal referred to by Sheila is an automatic connection and acceptance of the responsibility of parenting. There is a relationship or bond that the biological parent has with their child that the step-parent doesn't have and doesn't share. The relationship between step-parent and step-child has to have time to grow on its own, independent of the relationship between the married adults.

In the case of Lonnie and Sheila, both have skewed objectivity in their approach to Luke. Sheila tends to define her son's behaviors through her own struggles and experiences. Although empathy is important in parenting effectively, if not used appropriately it can be an excuse for not addressing behavior. A great quality Lonnie brings to the relationship is that he has objectivity and can see circumstances Sheila may have become blind to.

However, Lonnie must have the ability to effectively communicate his observations. Unfortunately, Lonnie is making a mistake that many step-parents make. Where he's assuming his assessment and way of handling the issue is accurate and more effective, he's not considering his position is only part of the entire picture of this family. He does not weigh the importance of a child's history as well as aspects of the child that he doesn't know or understand.

Lonnie and Sheila have two different perspectives on parenting. When blending families (or even with traditional families), this is an important conversation to have before the marriage. However, these conversations rarely happen.

Here, where the couple has already married, they are forced to arrive at a common plan that involves both biological parents and step-parents. Lonnie and Sheila have to treat each other's position as valid and equally as important in their attempts to parent. They have a history of parenting and goals of parenting that must be shared so that they can come to an agreement on methods and consequences. Having two separate perspectives, discipline methods, and goals in parenting will continue to build conflict and resentment towards each other. As a result, Lonnie will continue to insist that his way is better and Sheila will view her child's experiences through her own childhood memories.

Without productive conversation and parental agreement, Luke will eventually form an alliance with one parent and build bitterness toward the other. Consequently, his problems will not be adequately addressed. He will not have the benefit of appropriate solutions as long as his parents are unable to arrive at reasonable efforts to discover root causes and address Luke's problems. This will leave Luke with inadequate direction, emotional conflict, and entering adulthood without healthy living tools and decision-making skills.

This family will benefit from participating in a Blended Family group setting through their local church or

Christian counseling facility. They can benefit from hearing the successes and failures of families similar to their own. If group settings are not an option, family counseling is recommended. Also there are resources in Christian bookstores that offer engaging family activities and studies that promote wellness in blended families.

Step-parenting is not for the faint of heart. Thankfully, we have a God who is willing and able to help us through even the toughest parenting situations. With as many children as God has lovingly adopted into His family through Christ, surely He has remedies to reveal when we ask.

17 – Longsuffering

Couple: Calvin and Jerissa Hempstead
Married: 13 years
Children: Taylor (son) – age 10

Calvin dreaded showing the note to Jerissa, but there was no way around it. She took Taylor to soccer practice on Thursdays, so she needed the information. Still. Showing her the note on Monday would only mean an extra two days worth of Jerissa fussing and complaining about the revised snack schedule. Quite frankly, Calvin didn't want to hear Jerissa's mouth.

He shoved the note about snacks into his pocket while grabbing Taylor's bag filled with more than any ten-year-old needed at a soccer practice. Jerissa had packed two bottles of Gatorade (different flavors to suit Taylor), a first-aid kit, a flashlight, an extra pair of socks (in case the ones from school were too dirty), hand sanitizer, and biodegradable hand-wipes.

"It's only an hour-long soccer practice," Calvin had remarked after he'd questioned the weight of the bag and she'd explained its contents.

"You never know what will happen. I'd rather you be over-prepared than underprepared."

On one hand, Calvin loved the fact Jerissa was so conscientious. When they were in college, she helped him keep track of his assignments and due dates. She'd created a spreadsheet to help him live off a budget so that he wouldn't run out of money before the end of the semester. She'd been a great help, which (aside from her beautiful face) was what he thought he'd wanted in a wife.

But from the moment he'd asked her to marry him until now, fifteen years later, Jerissa's meticulous examination and over-preparation had taken on a life of its own and, in fact, grown more horrendous with time.

When their son, Taylor, was born, Calvin had hoped that Jerissa would calm down. Surely, having a baby around the house would improve Jerissa's patience and flexibility.

Wrong. Taylor's birth only made things worse—if that were possible.

Calvin could only imagine what Taylor's upcoming rebellious teenage years might hold in store for their family. Thus far, Taylor had been a model son. But it was only a matter of time before he began to test the waters in the process of transforming into a young man.

Calvin made small-talk with Taylor on the way home from soccer practice. This was a sacred time for them—an opportunity to express themselves without Jerissa's interruption.

But of course the time was short-lived. When they entered the garage, Calvin reminded Taylor to take off his shoes and leave them on the mat outside the door.

"Yes sir," Taylor replied obediently.

They entered the house and immediately Jerissa began running the show. "Taylor, leave your planner open to this week so I can check it. Calvin, there's mail for you on the coffee table. Dinner's in fifteen minutes," she yelled from the kitchen.

"Yeah. Thanks," Calvin said, grabbing the envelope Jerissa mentioned. It was from his Aunt Jane in Houston. He broke the seal and unfolded the letter. *It's Family Reunion Time!*

A smile crept across his face as he read through the details of the upcoming reunion. The thought of seeing his cousins, uncles, and aunts brought back warm memories of yesteryear—back when his life had been fresh, new, and full of possibilities. He also looked forward to introducing Taylor to people he'd never met.

"What's that?" Jerissa looked over his shoulder.

"Family reunion." He turned and handed her the letter.

"July? In Houston? Are they crazy? Don't they know how hot it will be in Texas by then?"

"Looks like they're doing it inside at a recreation center for the most part." Calvin pointed at the location listed on the page.

"It's still too hot for traveling." Jerissa shook her head. She flipped to the back side. "Twenty-five dollars per person, including T-shirts? Really? Why is it so cheap? What are we going to eat all weekend—hot dogs and chips? Who's planning this?"

"I'm guessing Aunt Jane."

Jerissa shook her head. "I swear, if they have us starving outside in the heat...." She dropped the paper on the table. "How did practice go?"

"Good."

Jerissa propped her hands on her hips. "Did he give Taylor a chance to practice?"

"Yeah. All the kids practiced."

"No. You have to watch the coach. He has favorites. And he tried to make Taylor play goalie last week."

Jerissa took off for the kitchen again as Calvin followed.

"What's wrong with goalie?"

"Seriously?" She stirred cheese into the macaroni. "Why won't he make *his* son play goalie? No one wants to be goalie. You don't really get to do anything. How's Taylor supposed to build up his skills if all he does is stand around for most of the game?"

"Someone has to tend the goal," Calvin challenged slightly.

"Not my kid. I'll have a talk with the coach Thursday."

The timer went off on the oven. "I'll get it," Calvin offered.

"No. Step back." Jerissa shooed him away. She grabbed the potholders from an adjacent drawer and carefully pulled the baked chicken breasts from the oven. "Awesome sauce!"

Calvin had to admit to himself the food did look quite delicious. Sometimes, Jerissa's penchant for perfection paid off.

She stepped into the hallway. "Dinner's ready!"

Taylor came bounding toward the table, and they sat to eat.

Calvin said grace and Jerissa dished the food out to Calvin and Taylor first, then herself.

"Taylor, sit up straight," she ordered.

Instantly, his back stiffened.

"So what's this whole goalie thing?"

"Coach says I have good hands," Taylor said proudly.

"No. He's just saying that to get over on you. You're the *best*, Taylor. You should be up front scoring points."

"But I like being goalie. I mean, you get to stop the *other* team from scoring. Defense wins games."

"That's a good way to put it," Calvin said.

Jerissa gave her husband the evil-eye. "Like I said. I'll be talking to the coach."

"No, Mom. Please don't."

"Taylor, you can't let people run over you! You have to stand up for yourself. Otherwise, people will take advantage of you."

"I'll talk to him myself," Taylor said.

Jerissa sat back in her chair. "You?"

"Yes. I can do it."

Calvin couldn't have been more proud of his son.

He reached over Taylor and grabbed the salt and pepper, dashing extra flavor onto the chicken.

"You're putting too much salt on the chicken," Jerissa scolded.

"It's my chicken. My palate."

"Fine." She sighed. "Don't come crawling to me when you're having a heart attack."

"Don't speak those words over me. I'm *not* going to have a heart attack."

"You will if you keep adding salt to everything," she whipped back. "You have to be more responsible with your health."

Calvin wanted to add a few more sprinkles, but didn't want to hear Jerissa's mouth anymore. Eating lightly-seasoned chicken was far better than the bitterness of his wife's negativity.

The next lines of conversation proved no sweeter. Jerissa fussed about her sister's new car (it was too expensive), the pastor's email (he failed to mention the women's conference), and the neighbor's puppy (they had taken the poor thing away from its mother too soon).

Calvin knew from experience there was no use confronting her, though. More often than not, Jerissa's assertions proved correct.

She just had a way of making everyone else suffer long and hard in the meantime.

Longsuffering
Counselor's Commentary

How do you get to the place of assuming the responsibility for the actions of the entire family? How do you get to the point of making sure others in the family think, behave, and make decisions to your approval? You control and demand that they do. Jerissa has taken the concept of scripts to a different level. She doesn't get upset when people go off-script. Instead, Jerissa prevents the coup by playing her part and demanding others play their part, too.

For Jerissa, and others like her, this isn't a conscientious decision. It's a response to stressful situations, fear, and may have been a modus operandi for long before the marriage. Initially, Calvin appreciated Jerissa's personality and appreciated her intelligence, confidence, and decisiveness. After thirteen years, however, she has become pushy and controlling.

Jerissa probably doesn't see herself as controlling or demanding. But when it is identified, she becomes defensive and tends to state her intentions, as though her intentions outweigh anyone's opinion. If we asked Jerissa, she would probably say that she's trying to make sure their marriage or their family work and that she wants to ensure her son is strong and knows how to stand up for himself. She thinks she is being helpful, filling a need, or giving the gift of her knowledge and experience and will dismiss any objections to her behavior and label them as complaints and her not being appreciated.

She may have little knowledge or comprehension of how her behavior affects her husband or child. She will not see the feelings of resentment that fuel their decisions to not respond or to acquiesce in order to avoid retaliation because of their objection or differing opinion. Unfortunately, whether she means to or not, she communicates to her family that they are not competent. She comes across as demeaning and unsupportive.

Is this her intent? Probably not. She may have had life experiences that have led to her decision to "take the reigns" or "someone's gotta do it."

However, if we ask "What is it like to be married to me?" or "How would I feel if I were treated like I treat my spouse or family?" we may begin to develop insight into how we are impacting our loved ones and begin to develop empathy which will change our behavior. Many of us do not want our spouses to feel inadequate, unsupported, controlled, or demeaned.

Ephesians 4:29 reads, "Let no corrupt communication proceed out of your mouth but that which is good to the use of edifying, that it may minister grace unto the hearers."

It is our responsibility to care for each other in our communications. Regardless of Jerissa's intentions, it is her obligation to build up her family through her actions and words. Although she may perceive herself as helpful, it is imperative that she listens to her family and notices their responses during her interactions.

To be on the receiving end of a controlling or demanding spouse is hurtful and may lead to angry outbursts, resentment, emotional shutdowns, or turning outside of the marriage for feelings of comfort and support. These responses aren't helpful or beneficial to the relationship, either. One's choice in responding to the controlling spouse is always their responsibility. It's important to communicate the impact of their behavior by talking when things are calm and there is no conflict. Ephesians 4:29 should also be recalled as they state their feelings and work toward change.

Remember the "Jerissa" spouse honestly believes that their intentions are for good. When one makes the decision to go off-script, they should simply say, "I would like to do it my way this time," or "Thank you. I wish to approach it differently." This may take a while but consistency is important regardless of the response.

As with all marital issues, care must be taken to approach this one with love and consideration. Believers are called to be submissive toward one another. Submission is something we give—not something to be snatched from another's trembling hands. Prayerful consideration of the inclusion of a Christian therapist who can teach how to bring the model of mutual submission into a marriage may prove helpful. Without intervention, a nagging spouse left unchecked will only get worse.

18 - Bullying Parent

Couple: James and Megan Abernathy
Married: 20 years
Children: Rico – age 20; Jacquelyn – age 17

Diary,
I don't know how I picked this man for a dad for my kids. I must have been delusional.

So, here goes: Jacquelyn and her friend wanted to go to a cancer walk at a major league ballpark roughly 25 minutes away. The walk started at 7pm and would last through 7am. She and her friend weren't actually walking, but they were going to be on the sidelines handing cups of water to the walkers and cheering them on. I told her she could go, but she needed to be home by her regular curfew.

Anyway, I went to eat dinner with Alice. Jacquelyn called me around 9 and asked me to talk to James because he wouldn't let her go to the walk (she and her friend were already at my house preparing to leave). Calling the absent parent to intervene is normally a no-no, but since I figured it was a matter of lack of miscommunication from me to him, I let her put him on the phone. I told James that Jacquelyn and I already discussed this, and it was okay with me.

He said it wasn't okay with him because he'd never heard of an all-night cancer marathon. He vetoed the plan.

My daughter took her friend back home, I went back to enjoying dinner with Alice—or at least I tried to.

When I got home, James fussed at me for being so naïve about what "this girl" is up to. He says the whole thing sounds fishy and I should have known better. "There's no such thing as an all-night cancer walk. Don't you recognize a teenager's lie when you hear it?"

So I went online, pulled up this obnoxiously massive website about the 12-hour cancer walk. I even showed him pictures of my FaceBook friends who were at the walk that very moment.

He grumbled, "Well, it was too late for them to be leaving the house anyway."

This was when I got angry and the evil thoughts came rushing from my heart, straight up through my mouth. "First of all, you don't do anything charitable, you know nothing about charitable events. So the fact that you've never heard of an all-night cancer walk means absolutely nothing.

"Secondly, it would have taken you two seconds—two seconds— to Google and find out if there was such an event.

"Thirdly, our daughter is leaving for college in three months. If she doesn't know how to conduct herself like a young lady by now, we're in deep trouble, buddy.

"Fourthly, how dare you question my parenting skills when you've left most of the hard work up to me all these years!

I could go on. Fifthly, sixthly...nineteenthly.

But it wouldn't change anything. As I see it, he was being a bully, playing the "Daddy" card because he could, viewing life through his usual negatively shaded, distrustful lenses. Now, if our daughter had a history of lying or sneaking out, if she wasn't keeping her grades up at school, or if she hadn't exhibited enough responsibility to be promoted to a shift manager at her job, I could understand James's position. Jacquelyn is not a perfect child, but on the rare occasions that she has made a wrong decision, she's owned up and faced the consequences. Far more than James's own mother would say about him at age 17!!!

What hurts more than anything is to see how this affects our kids. At this point, I think both Rico and Jacquelyn have decided that their dad is unreasonable and cannot be taken seriously. They respect his position, just as I do. But they don't respect him as a person, and I can't say that I blame them.

-Megan

Bullying Parent
Counselor's Commentary

So many of us are desperately trying to make sense of our lives. We are trying to become better people. Better wives. Better husbands. Better parents. We read. We talk with friends. We go to our church. We go to counseling. We want to be better. In our attempt to fill ourselves with new information, sometimes we miss the fact that we are filled with so many experiences, memories, and details that already impact us. So many occurrences in our lives have formed our personality, thoughts, and ability to form relationships.

All of our experiences and information that have made us who we are continue to impact our ability to parent our children well. We all want the absolute best for our precious little ones. We often form our parental rules based on our experiences as children ourselves. While media and later experiences can impact our ideas about rearing children, people underestimate the reality of how much all of these experiences form the basis of our relationship with our own kids.

Some of us want to raise our children similar to how our parents raised us. Or, depending on our experiences, we tend to steer opposite of them. Either way, we parent with a reference to how we were parented as our starting point.

Regardless of our own childhood and how we were parented, we must remember that our children are not us nor do they have our parents. Even though we made certain decisions and were influenced by certain people, it does not mean that our children will make the same decisions or mistakes. Although our parents had reasons for their decisions and circumstances, our children have us. They are growing up in different circumstances as well as a different day and time. Does this mean that we should throw out our parenting knowledge and revamp our beliefs in parenting? No. Should we adopt a worldly perspective and treat our children as little adults? Certainly not. Many of us have a rich history of great parenting and want to pass it on to our children.

What we want to make sure we do, regardless of our background, is be sure our approaches are tailored to each child, their personality, and their needs.

Megan and James have several issues that are impacting their ability to parent effectively. Their lack of communication, distrust, and conflictual communication greatly influence not only their parenting, but it impacts their children's relationship with them.

Our relationships with our spouses have great influence on our children's ability to love and give love. They often model the healthy and unhealthy aspects of our marriages. We must be fully aware of how we treat each other because our model establishes our children's rules for love and parenting. The responsibility of providing a healthy example of love and Godly parenting is shared by both spouses. Despite all our lectures and verbal warnings, children rarely respond to what they are told but hugely demonstrate what they see.

Unfortunately in this situation, James may have a history of experiences, mistakes, and fears that lead him to parent through these experiences and with an authoritarian style. Often parents who parent with this style are rule-oriented and considered strict. They love their children dearly and will often voice their aim is to protect their children. Regrettably, children tend to respond only to their authority and often lack relationships with this type of parent.

Parents are considered bullies when they exhibit aggression and inability to parent with empathy and understanding. They use threats, punishments, and their position to control behavior, thereby fostering an environment that does not cultivate healthy parent/child relationships. In this situation, James has insinuated that his daughter is dishonest without allowing room for discussion or understanding. As a result, he was unable to appreciate his daughter's desire to positively impact her community. This can have long-term effects on his daughter's desire to establish a close relationship with him or healthy relationships with men.

God's Word specifically addresses aggression in parenting. Ephesians 6:4 warns, "Fathers, do not provoke your children to anger, but bring them up in the discipline and instruction of the Lord."

Often, we ask men or women who are aggressive in their approach to parenting, "Are you the man or woman you want your daughter or son to marry? Are you the parents you want your children to become? Are you the example of love, forgiveness, mercy, and grace that is extended to you daily?" These questions often invoke personal assessment, but rarely a response.

Megan can attempt to have a discussion with James regarding his approach to their children. Acknowledging her understanding of his attempts of protecting them and raising them to be responsible adults is very important. Establishing a common goal of caring for their children, instead of setting up an accusatory environment, can help make sure the conversation is productive. Also, having a family meeting that includes Megan, James, and their kids can help provide clarity of expectations and establish trust. Meetings should not be gripe sessions but purposed in understanding, healthy communication, and resolution. This can be a great place to voice concerns, resolve conflict and discuss expectations. Regular family meetings can strengthen family bonds and foster feelings of togetherness.

Parenting should be a practice that involves empathy, relationship, respect, choice, and consequences that are appropriate. It is a team effort with parents who can effectively communicate and share a common goal. That goal is to raise healthy responsible children who are able to love, receive love, form healthy relationships, make productive choices, and live a life in Christ! We are charged in Titus 2:7, "Show yourself in all respects to be a model of good works, and in your teaching show integrity, dignity…"

19 - Just Financially Wrong

Couple: Artemis and Victoria Jones
Married: 10 years
Children: Olivia – age 6

After a long, frustrating, pointless meeting at work, Victoria needed a drink—except she didn't drink, which meant she needed something else to calm her nerves. Sometimes she wished she did like alcohol, then she'd have an easy fix.

Instead, she called her best friend, Maya, and vented everything she'd kept bottled inside during the four-hour team conference. "They're driving me crazy! Everything they said could have been conveyed in a five minute email. It's like they all want to hear themselves talk."

"Now Victoria, you know what the problem is, right?"

"No. What?" She put the key in the ignition of her Benz and checked all mirrors before backing out of her parking space.

"The problem is that people don't read their email messages."

"The world is full of nincompoops. I have *got* to get another job."

"Really, Victoria?"

"Yes. Really. I'll go insane if I keep working at this place."

"Umm…and what would Artemis have to say about you quitting another job?"

Victoria rolled her eyes as though Maya could see her. "He'd have a cow."

"Right."

"But I wouldn't quit unless I had another one lined up. Happy?"

"Girl, you are a mess." Maya laughed.

While waiting for a light to change, Victoria checked her email again. A coupon for Josephina's Fashions popped up on the screen. *50% OFF ONE ITEM – TODAY ONLY!* Already, Victoria felt her mood elevating.

"Hello?"

"Oh. I'm sorry. I gotta go. I'll call you later."

"Okay. Take it easy. And don't quit your job, Victoria. Remember the goals you and Artemis set to pay off debt so my goddaughter can go to college."

"Yeah. Yeah. College, shmollege. I gotta go. Bye."

Now that Victoria had gotten little-Miss-budget off the phone, she could concentrate on more important things like getting to the store before the sale ended.

Thirty minutes, two sweaters, one pair of shiny gold pants, and a bracelet purchase later, Victoria walked out of the store. Her heart pounded with satisfaction. Yes, she'd spent more than she'd planned, but she'd also saved almost seventy dollars.

She rushed to pick up her daughter before the daycare closed. Thanks to the shopping detour, she didn't have time to cook. Instead, she called ahead and ordered two entrees and a kids' meal at a local Italian restaurant. She picked up the food and joyfully traveled on home with the sight of the plastic garment bags draped across the passenger's seat winking back at her.

Artemis called on his 7:00 pm break as he always did. "Babe?"

"Hey."

"I'm looking at the checking account."

Uh oh. "Yeah."

"Josephina's Fashions?"

"Oh. Well, I picked up a cute bracelet for Olivia, too. And I had a coupon."

"Yeah, but you managed to spend almost half of what you make in a week."

She hadn't thought of it that way. "The coupon—"

"And then you went out to eat?"

"No. I brought it *home*," she corrected him. "Olivia and I do have to eat, you know?"

"But this is *not* what we discussed," Artemis fussed. "We agreed on a plan. A budget. A goal."

"Look, I work hard every day, okay? I deserve to enjoy life," Victoria reminded herself and her husband.

"I work hard, too, but you don't see me spending money like crazy, do you? Driving around in a Benz but can't afford to put gas in the tank on Thursdays," he chided.

Victoria stopped twirling her pasta. "Whatever. I'm not going to keep arguing with you about my car."

"I still don't know what possessed you to go there. We still can't afford it."

"Life is short, Artemis. I've wanted a Benz ever since I was a little girl. I'm almost thirty-five years old now. You think I want to be *fifty* before I can have the finer things in life?"

"It's not about you. It's about Olivia," Artemis said in a begging tone.

"Olivia needs to see that hard work pays off," Victoria reasoned. "Plus, God rewards those that love Him. We're His children. We deserve the best."

She heard Artemis sigh. "I can't with you."

"I can't with you, either."

"Bye."

"Bye."

Just Financially Wrong
Counselor's Commentary

Falling in love and deciding to marry is a wonderful endeavor. However, it is irresponsible to think that healthy marriages are built only on love and love is all that matters. If this romantic notion were an actuality, divorce rates would be minimal.

We have all heard that financial conflict is the number one cause for divorce. Premarital counseling, marriage experts, financial experts, and even statistics have warned us about the importance of finances in relationships. Still, we often fail to get a true understanding of the spending and saving habits of our prospective spouses before we say "I do." We think that the financial meeting of the minds can come later or that a potential spouse's unhealthy habits will eventually change. We behave as if togetherness in other areas of the relationship will facilitate togetherness financially. Wouldn't that be great?

While it is important that we aim for partnership and connectivity, it is also important to discuss and develop financial plans and goals. Some questions to consider:

- What is the plan for saving? Investment? Retirement?
- What are our views on sharing an account?
- What do we believe regarding oneness in finances?

- What is your income?
- What is the monthly budget?
- What are our debts?
- What are our credit scores?
- How much do we give to church/charities?
- Are we willing/able to financially support parent(s) as they age if necessary? If so, how much?
- Will we both continue to work if/when we have children?
- How much is too much to spend without consulting each other?
- What about our children's education—public or private schools? Are we contributing to their college expenses or do we believe that paying for college is their personal responsibility?
- Do we give allowances to our kids? Do we reward our kids with money for good grades?

As we establish these plans, we must first question our own financial framework and how we developed our financial intelligence. What were we taught about spending or saving? What is our emotional attachment to money? What is our definition of success?

It appears as though Victoria previously developed an idea that identity, self-worth, and contentment can be created and maintained through financial achievement and visual evidence of that success. She has also created temporary emotional gratification through shopping.

Unfortunately, this will only provide short-lived feelings of satisfaction and elation. These feelings often quickly spiral down into remorse, sadness, and sometimes guilt. The "fix" for Victoria being down in the dumps is to shop some more.

As we see in the case of Victoria and Artemis, this cycle leads to frustration and conflict. Victoria's attitude could be a result of financial struggles as a child or affluence without financial guidance. Due to her lack of insight, Victoria has justified her actions and refuses to honor the plan and goals of her family. Inadvertently, she has created division and mistrust. The realization she's not alone and her life's no longer about just her is paramount. She is not only causing difficulty in her marriage, she's also making temporary decisions that will impact their daughter in a few years when she's preparing to enter college.

Like many of the couples we've visited in this book, Victoria and Artemis could use some intervention. Artemis has already tried to reason with her, as evidenced by the plans they previously agreed to before Victoria blew the budget with an impromptu shopping spree. They're in need of an objective eye to help them through this season in their marriage. This can be an exercise in partnership by enrolling in a financial planning class or counseling together. These classes are beneficial as they can help both Artemis and Victoria voice their financial perspectives, establish goals, and equip them to meet them. As a result, they both can feel supported and experience less stress associated with their financial habits.

20 - Living Separate Lives

Couple: Joshua and Cammie Gilbert
Married: 3 years

Driving to the grocery store, Cammie called her friend, Elizabeth. "Hey, girl."

"Hey, Cam. What's up?"

"Shopping."

Elizabeth shrieked, "Why didn't you tell me?"

"It's not *fun* shopping. Just food and household items."

"That is so cute. Look at you, happy little homemaker."

"Whatever!" Cammie snagged a parking spot near the grocery store's entrance. "It's not as glamorous as it seems."

"Oh, please. You were like Miss-I-Wanna-Get-Married for three years before you met Joshua."

"It's good. I'm just sayin', it ain't as good as my grandmomma's greens and hotwater cornbread."

Elizabeth busted out laughing. "You are crazy."

Their easy conversation continued as Cammie made her rounds up and down aisles, filling her basket with her favorite entrees, sides, desserts, and drinks. She also stopped to pick up feminine products and toiletries.

She and Elizabeth yapped all through the checkout and even as Cammie pulled up to a drive-through at Mickey D's. "Hold on."

After she finished the order for a double cheeseburger meal, she returned to the conversation. "I'm back."

"Wait, why are you ordering fast food when you just went grocery shopping?"

"I don't feel like cooking today."

"So what's Joshua going to eat?"

Cammie snapped playfully, "I don't know. I guess whatever his two hands make." Her phone buzzed. "Speaking of the devil, that's him calling."

"Okay. Call me back?"

Cammie pressed the red reject button to send Joshua's call to voice mail. "I'll talk to him later. So what are you up to these days?"

Elizabeth rattled off a list of her endeavors: writing another book, planning a vacation to Hawaii, rehearsing for a part in her church's play. She shared short snippets of information about each upcoming adventure.

"Girl, you've got a busy schedule these days?"

"Probably not any busier than you," Elizabeth downplayed it.

By then, Cammie had gotten her food and returned to hers and Joshua's apartment. She walked past him as he played video games, straight on to their kitchen where she put away the groceries. She proceeded to the bedroom to store the toiletries, all the while continuing the conversation with Elizabeth. "So what are you doing tonight?"

"Going to the opening night of the women's conference at Jenn's church."

"Really? How is she? Who's speaking?"

"Jenn is good. And I don't know who's speaking. I think tonight is kind of the opening night. It's free. Lots of singing, and they have a Christian comedian coming. We're just getting out of the house to have some girl-time. You want to come?"

"Yes! Girl, you know I do!" Cammie laughed. "What time?"

"Seven."

"Cool. I'll be at your house in forty-five minutes."

She ended the call with Elizabeth and rushed to her closet to find the perfect attire. An oversized sweater, skinny jeans, and a pair of boots were always appropriate this time of year. She couldn't wait to hang out with her college friends again and enjoy the conference.

After a quick shower, changing clothes, and gulping down her food, Cammie breezed past Joshua. "I'm going to a conference with Elizabeth and Jenn."

"Bye," he grunted.

"Yeah."

Living Separate Lives
Counselor's Commentary

What is really going on with Cammie and Joshua?

What we have to address first is the overarching lack of regard and concern for their marriage and each other. Throughout the scenario, Cammie displays this disregard by having more interest in her activities and friends than her husband. She had many opportunities to engage with him. Refusing his phone call, not bringing him food, not being interested in him when she arrived, and spending the evening with her friends instead of him were all missed opportunities for nourishing her marriage and connecting with Joshua.

We know some may disagree and blame Joshua's gaming. That is also an issue that shouldn't be ignored. He has just as much responsibility for the separateness of the relationship as she does. It is human nature to look to someone other than ourselves to hold the majority of the responsibility when we spot problems. We look to point to someone or something else in order to relieve our feelings of possibly being the cause of the separation.

Let's talk truth. When we first marry, we start out excited about our lives together. We have plans that we think no one can interrupt. We cuddle under blankets as we watch our favorite shows. We look forward to coming home to be with one another. We even refuse to make plans without the other.

Then there does come a time when our schedules and activities of the day become routine and our newlywed feelings fade. Children are born. There are job changes and situation changes. We change. Unfortunately, we underestimate the complexities of life and the impact of our own feelings and behaviors on our marriage. We unknowingly start to drift apart and fail to deliberately create situations that promote togetherness. If we are not intentionally investing and constantly praying for each other in our marriages, we can get to a place of complacency. We then allow other situations, people, and interests to take place and erode our feelings of togetherness.

We regularly ask when we come into contact with couples who have separate lives and interests, "Why are you married? What's the point?" The Bible teaches that two should become one. We must stop and ask ourselves, "How can we become one living separately? How are your actions impacting the oneness of your relationship? What are you doing to make sure your spouse is well cared for and is growing as a result of being married to you? How would you feel being married to you in this situation?"

So yes, Cammie and Joshua have a situation where complacency and disregard have ruled. However, it would be irresponsible to think this issue has only to do with different interests. What we have to understand is that marriages are doing one of two things regarding a sense of connectedness and growth. We are either getting better or worse. We are not marking time and remaining the same.

In this situation, each time they pass each other, it broadens the gap. Each time they do things separate they allow room for other people and things to pull them away from each other. In marriages, both men and women want the same thing—a feeling of connectedness and support.

We beg for it. We argue for it. We mostly want to be heard and understood. We will try different ways to communicate this. We have many unspoken expectations. Some we're aware of and others we're not. When we feel that these expectations aren't being met, we normally put up walls of protection. We don't want to feel vulnerable to someone we think doesn't want the same thing. Unfortunately, you eventually take care of and protect your heart and have little regard for how your actions are impacting your spouse.

One of the biggest mistakes in marriages is to assume that ours is the only and the most important experience. We hand our life lenses over to the other and expect them to have the same view. However, we have so many life experiences that have made us who we are. Our childhood, parents, friends, school, and our spiritual maturity influence how we exist in our marriages. We are complicated to ourselves. It is unfortunate that we don't allow time for our spouses to learn us. We are expecting the other to immediately understand our expectations and successfully meet them. We offer little room for error.

But there is hope!

We have to first acknowledge there is a problem. A good rule of healthy engagement is to admit our own contributions to the feelings of disconnect and offer ways we are willing to grow. It takes emotional maturity and personal insight in order to do this. If one or both are not able to engage healthily, there are feelings and statements like, "Why do I have to be the one? Why can't he or she admit *their* faults first? I only respond to *their* faults. I am not the one who is doing the most damage." But as soon as one person reaches the point where they are able to move past these sentiments, that person is in the best position to initiate change.

We must learn to take care of our spouses in our communication and our responses. This means to actively listen with our ears, eyes, and hearts. We must empathically relate to their experience in the marriage and attempt to care for them emotionally and behaviorally. We may not understand or agree with their experience. However, it is theirs and we must acknowledge it.

In addition, we have to be able to voice expectations and be willing to meet the other's needs. We can learn to focus on the impact of behaviors rather than what we feel are shortcomings of the other.

We can do this by using "When/I feel" statements. Joshua might benefit from saying, "When you spend more time with your friends than me, I feel disregarded and alone."

Cammie can state her experience as well. "When you are playing your game, I feel as though I am not enough." This can open the door for healthy engagement that places importance on changing behaviors rather than trying to blame and change each other.

Our choices to be happy and content are our own. It is not the responsibility of our spouses. However, it is our responsibility to nurture and care for each other with the intensity in which we expect and that Christ does for us!

Discussion/Reflection Questions

1. Do you think Jada was over-reacting or that her husband, Evan, was under-reacting about what took place with their daughter at Daniyah's house?
2. Jada and Evan have some unresolved in-law issues from the past. How are those contributing to the current disagreement?
3. Do you think Sheila should allow Lonnie to discipline Luke for making a bad grade in math?
4. Is Sheila making excuses for Luke?
5. Would Lonnie and Sheila's situation be much different if Lonnie were Luke's biological father? How so?
6. Calvin dreads Taylor's teen years because he thinks Taylor will become rebellious due to Jerissa's controlling behavior. Do you think Calvin's fears are well-founded? Is it biblical for believers to expect their teens to be rebellious, or is this a western experience that we have adopted as truth?
7. One might compare Jerissa to Martha in Luke 10:38-42. How are they similar? How are they different?
8. Jerissa means well. Why are her good intentions perceived so negatively?
9. Did you perceive James as too strict? Did you perceive Megan as too lenient?
10. The response to "The Bullying Parent" states that we parent with our own parents in mind. How were you

taught, trained, and disciplined? Do you or would you do anything differently with a child in your care?

11. Victoria has blown the budget in order to experience a "shopping high". Is turning to shopping any different than turning to a substance for a temporary fix?

12. Victoria believes that life is short and those who work hard and love God should have something to show for all their hard work. Do you agree or disagree?

13. Cammie and Joshua are living two separate lives in their new marriage. How might Cammie's former days of living independently be impacting her decisions as a wife now?

14. How do you interpret Cammie's actions and words toward her husband? What about his actions and words toward her?

15. In Titus 2, believers are told that the older wives should mentor the younger wives. Why do you think this is important? Do you have a "wife" mentor? Have you ever mentored a younger wife?

16. Which commentary from the counselor stuck with you most?

Scriptures for Meditation

Trust in the Lord with all your heart
and lean not on your own understanding;
in all your ways submit to him,
and he will make your paths straight.
Proverbs 3:5-6

Whoever dwells in the shelter of the Most High
will rest in the shadow of the Almighty.
I will say of the Lord, "He is my refuge and my fortress,
my God, in whom I trust."
Surely he will save you
from the fowler's snare
and from the deadly pestilence.
He will cover you with his feathers,
and under his wings you will find refuge;
his faithfulness will be your shield and rampart.
You will not fear the terror of night,
nor the arrow that flies by day,
nor the pestilence that stalks in the darkness,
nor the plague that destroys at midday.
A thousand may fall at your side,
ten thousand at your right hand,
but it will not come near you.
You will only observe with your eyes
and see the punishment of the wicked.

If you say, "The Lord is my refuge,"
and you make the Most High your dwelling,
no harm will overtake you,
no disaster will come near your tent.
Psalm 91:1-10

Call to me and I will answer you and tell you great and
unsearchable things you do not know.'
Jeremiah 33:3

The wise store up choice food and olive oil,
but fools gulp theirs down.
Proverbs 21:20

Keep your lives free from the love of money and be
content with what you have, because God has said,
"Never will I leave you;
never will I forsake you."
Hebrews 13:5

For this reason a man will leave his father and mother and
be united to his wife, and the two will become one flesh.
Ephesians 5:31

Commit your work to the Lord, and your plans will be
established.
Proverbs 16:3

Do not be conformed to this world, but be transformed by
the renewal of your mind, that by testing you may discern

what is the will of God, what is good and acceptable and
perfect.
Romans 12:2

See to it that no one takes you captive by philosophy and
empty deceit, according to human tradition, according to
the elemental spirits of the world, and not according to
Christ.
Colossians 2:8

What therefore God has joined together, let not man
separate
Mark 10:9

Let no corrupting talk come out of your mouths, but only
such as is good for building up, as fits the occasion, that it
may give grace to those who hear.
Ephesians 4:29

Section Notes

Resources

Books

Fervent: A Women's Battle Plan for Serious, Specific, and Strategic Prayer by Priscilla Shirer

How to Pray for Your Children by Quin Sherrer and Ruthanne Garlock

Lies Women Believe: And the Truth that Sets Them Free by Nancy Leigh DeMoss

The Bait of Satan, 20th Anniversary Edition: Living Free from the Deadly Trap of Offense by John Bevere

The Excellent Wife: A Biblical Perspective by Martha Peace

The Holy Bible (your favorite version)

The Making of a Spiritual Warrior: A Woman's Guide to Daily Victory by Quin Sherrer and Ruthanne Garlock

The Power of a Praying Husband by Stormie Omartian

The Power of a Praying Wife by Stormie Omartian

Thriving Despite a Difficult Marriage by Michael Misja and Chuck Misja

Websites

FocusontheFamily.com

SquadronofSisters.com

WarriorWives.Club

About the Authors

Shundria Riddick

Shundria Riddick is a speaker and licensed professional counselor who shares a message of hope and freedom in Christ.

A graduate of Amberton University, Shundria holds a Master's Degree in Counseling. As a counselor, she loves to connect with individuals and seeks to guide them with biblical truth. This desire to walk beside those who are experiencing difficult seasons in their lives has given her a phenomenal ability to disarm any audience. Her passion is to help others grasp the unshakable love of Christ, let go of frustration that comes from trying to live out one's own plans and experience the beauty of embracing His will.

Like many women, she has a career, an advanced education, and is a successful wife and mother of three school-aged children. And like the typical woman, she has juggled all of these while dealing with the emotional and mental battles of life's daily issues. God has graciously given her the opportunity to share with women, singles, girls, and married couples as they seek to live out their victory in Christ.

Shundria is a wife to her best friend Chris and mother to three wonderful children, Joshua, Elyana and Noah.

Shundria works with clients in face-to-face and virtual counseling sessions.

Visit her online at www.ShundriaRiddick.com.

Michelle Stimpson

Bestselling author Michelle Stimpson has penned more than thirty Christian fiction books including traditional bestseller *Divas of Damascus Road*, Amazon #1 bestseller, *Stepping Down*, the award-winning Mama B series, and *Falling Into Grace*, which has been optioned for a made-for-TV movie. She has also published more than fifty short stories through her educational publishing company, WeGottaRead.com. Michelle holds an English degree from Jarvis Christian College and a Master's Degree in Education from the University of Texas at Arlington.

She is a part-time language arts consultant and serves in women's ministry through teaching and publishing. She and her husband have two young adult children and one bizarre dog.

Visit her online at www.MichelleStimpson.com.